Somatic Therapy Workbook (5 in 1)

Anika Sullivan

GRAPEVINE BOOKS

Published by
GRAPEVINE BOOKS

www.grapevinebooks.com
email: grapevineindiapublishers@gmail.com

Ordering Information:
Quantity sales: Special discounts are available on quantity purchases by corporations, associations, and others.
For details, reach out to the publisher.

First published by Grapevine Books, 2025

TABLE OF CONTENTS

TABLE OF **CONTENTS**

TABLE OF

CONTENTS

Somatic therapy is the art of reconnecting with the wisdom your body already holds.

INTRODUCTION

Imagine a polar bear, one of the most powerful apex predators in the animal kingdom, suddenly faced with a near-death experience. In the wild, this bear has never known fear, but now, trapped and immobilized, it is paralyzed with terror. As it inches closer to death, the bear's body begins to tremble uncontrollably. Its eyes shut, and its massive frame quivers from head to toe. This trembling is not a sign of weakness or panic; it is nature's way of helping the bear release the overwhelming energy from its traumatic experience. Within moments, the bear emerges, physically unharmed and psychologically intact, able to return to the wilderness as if the near-death experience never happened.

What this polar bear demonstrates is a profound biological truth: animals in the wild, despite facing life-threatening dangers, rarely suffer from long-term trauma. Their bodies instinctively know how to process and release the energy from a traumatic event, allowing them to reset and recover. After encountering stress, these animals shake, tremble, or take deep breaths, naturally healing their nervous systems and preventing the trauma from becoming locked in their bodies. In essence, they discharge the survival energy and return to a state of calm.

But what about humans? Why do so many of us—along with animals in captivity—carry the weight of trauma long after the event has passed? The answer lies in the way our modern lives interfere with this innate healing process. Unlike wild animals, humans have learned to suppress the natural responses to trauma, largely due to societal norms, conditioning, and the pressures to "stay composed." Instead of trembling or releasing the energy of a stressful event, we tighten up, push through, and carry on. Over time, this trapped energy becomes embedded in our nervous systems, manifesting as anxiety, depression, PTSD, chronic pain, and a host of other health issues.

This understanding led to the development of somatic therapy. It came into being when scientists and therapists began to notice that, unlike humans and zoo animals, wild animals don't develop psychological disorders after traumatic experiences. But by observing these natural processes, they also realized something profound. Our bodies have an innate ability to heal from trauma—if only we allow them to. Somatic therapy taps into this forgotten ability to release trauma, using biology, neuroscience, and psychology to restore balance to the nervous system.

At the core of somatic therapy is the autonomic nervous system (ANS), which controls our body's stress response. When we face trauma, the ANS shifts into a survival mode, preparing us to fight, flee, or freeze. However if the survival energy is not released, it remains trapped in the body, disrupting our overall health. In modern society, we rarely allow ourselves to process these responses fully, and over time, this trapped energy builds up, leading to conditions such as chronic fatigue, insomnia, heart disease, and an overall diminished sense of joy.

The three states of the nervous system are Social Engagement, Fight/Flight, and Freeze. Social Engagement includes feelings of safety, connection, curiosity, and compassion. Fight/Flight involves fear, anxiety, anger, and frustration as a response to stress. Freeze is characterized by shutdown, dissociation, numbness, and helplessness. A curved line marks the shift from activation to shutdown, while a wavy line represents natural emotional regulation in the Social Engagement state.

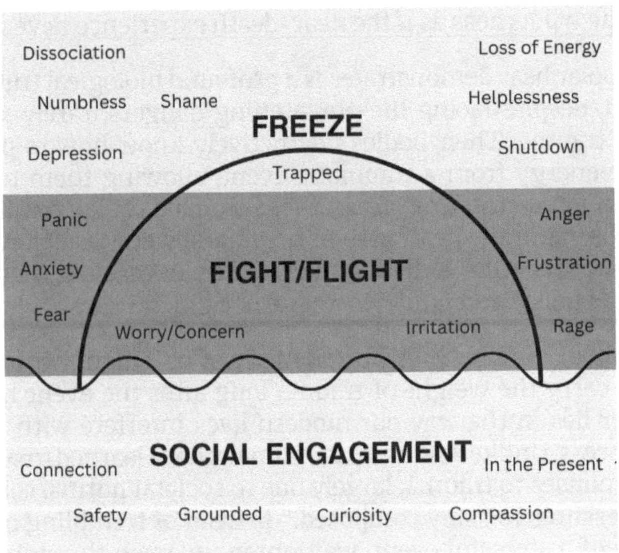

The key to healing through somatic therapy lies in reactivating the natural mechanisms within the ANS that release stored trauma. Rather than trying to "think" our way through trauma, which is the focus of many traditional therapies, somatic therapy works directly with the body's survival brain. By engaging the parasympathetic nervous system (PNS)—the branch of the ANS responsible for "rest and digest"—somatic therapy helps the body return to a state of calm, allowing natural healing processes to resume. In this parasympathetic state, the body produces acetylcholine, which regulates heart rate, reduces inflammation, and improves digestion, sleep, and immune function.

In essence, somatic therapy gives us the tools to complete the healing process that our bodies already know how to perform but have forgotten due to societal conditioning. Just as the polar bear trembles to release its trauma, somatic therapy helps us unlock that same healing potential within ourselves. The result is not only relief from trauma and stress but a deeper connection to our bodies' innate wisdom and resilience.

What led me here:

Growing up in the chaos of New York City, I had always been intrigued by the complexity of the human mind and emotions. My early career as a therapist focused on traditional talk therapy, helping clients navigate their pain through conversation, self-awareness, and cognitive restructuring. But deep down, I often felt that something was missing, especially for clients who seemed stuck, unable to move past their trauma no matter how much they understood it intellectually.

Then, one day, everything changed.

One of my clients, Sarah, had survived a serious car accident in her early twenties, but while her body had healed, something inside her hadn't. She would tense up every time she heard tires screeching. Even years later, she struggled with unexplained anxiety, chronic muscle tension, and restless sleep. She had gone through traditional therapy, learning to 'manage' her fears cognitively, but the physical distress remained.

During one of our therapy sessions, I guided Sarah to simply focus on the sensations in her body. At first, she was hesitant—like many of us, she had learned to suppress her physical reactions to fear. But as she stayed with the discomfort, something remarkable happened. Her shoulders started trembling, her breath deepened, and soon, she felt an overwhelming surge of energy move through her body. She wasn't reliving the accident; she was finally releasing the survival energy that had been trapped inside her for years. When the shaking subsided, she looked at me, wide-eyed, and whispered, "I feel... lighter." It was as if her body had been waiting all these years to complete what it never got to in that moment of trauma.

As I reflected on Sarah's experience, I began to see how deeply conditioned we are to suppress our natural responses to trauma. This realization was a turning point for me. I thought back to my clients struggling with anxiety, PTSD, and depression, and realized they, too, had survival energy stuck in their bodies. They had lost the natural ability to discharge this trauma—to let it go. I felt a deep pang of sadness for them—and for myself. It wasn't just my clients who had lost touch with this primal ability. I had been doing the same thing, unknowingly carrying my own unresolved emotions, even though I thought I had worked through them mentally.

That moment marked the beginning of my journey into somatic therapy. Determined to understand this further, I immersed myself in the study of the body, the autonomic nervous system, and how trauma becomes embedded within us. I learned that healing isn't just about understanding our trauma; it's about feeling it, allowing it to move through us, and physically releasing it.

One of the most powerful moments came during my training when I experienced somatic therapy firsthand. I had been carrying years of accumulated stress—both from my work as a therapist and my own personal struggles—without even realizing it. During one session, I was guided to simply focus on the sensations in my body, and without even trying, I began to shake. As my body trembled, I felt a surge of energy rise and then dissolve, like a tightly wound coil finally releasing. A deep sense of relief washed over me—like I had been holding my breath for years and was finally able to exhale.

It was then that I knew this was the path I needed to follow, not just for myself but for my clients. Somatic therapy goes beyond talking—it helps people reconnect with the wisdom of their bodies, allowing them to finally release the trauma they've been holding onto. It's a way to heal that we've forgotten, but one that is deeply rooted in our biology.

Now, as a somatic therapist, I feel honored to guide my clients through this profound process of healing. I know that real recovery doesn't just come from thinking about our trauma; it comes from feeling it, processing it, and ultimately, letting it go. We are all wired for healing. It's not something we need to learn—it's something we need to remember.

Why I recommend Somatic Therapy over other types of therapy:

Addresses the Root of Trauma: While traditional therapies focus on thoughts and emotions, somatic therapy directly engages with the body's stored trauma. By working with the nervous system, you can release trapped energy that talking alone cannot access.

Holistic Healing: Somatic therapy doesn't just treat the mind alone, but considers the body and its response to trauma. This integrative approach leads to deeper and more comprehensive healing, compared to therapies that focus solely on cognitive or emotional aspects.

Resolves Physical Symptoms: Many clients who suffer from trauma also experience physical symptoms like chronic pain, fatigue, or insomnia. Somatic therapy addresses the underlying nervous system dysregulation that causes these issues, leading to improved physical health alongside emotional well-being.

Sustainable Results: Somatic therapy teaches you how to tap into your body's natural ability to heal, creating long-term resilience. By learning how to regulate their nervous system, you develop tools you can use throughout your lives, leading to sustainable recovery.

Releases Stored Trauma: In my experience, talk therapy can sometimes lead to over-analysis, causing clients to revisit their trauma without fully releasing it. However, somatic therapy works to physically release the trauma stored in the body. This prevents re-traumatization and creates a sense of completion in the healing process.

Improves Emotional Regulation: By working directly with the autonomic nervous system, somatic therapy helps you improve your ability to manage stress and regulate emotions, resulting in a greater sense of stability and well-being.

Deeper Progress & Reduced Relapse: Many of my clients reported feeling profound shifts after just a few sessions of somatic therapy. It taps into the body's natural healing mechanism, allowing for quicker breakthroughs compared to the often slower progress of cognitive-based therapies.

What this book covers: the five core aspects of Somatic Therapy

After years of working with clients, witnessing profound transformations, and understanding the deep connection between the body and mind, I have chosen five key topics to form the foundation of this book: Healing, Toolbox, Exercises, Coping Skills, and Yoga. These topics were selected with care, each representing a crucial element of the somatic experience. Together, they form a path for readers—whether therapists, clients, or seekers of personal growth—to embody deeper awareness, resilience, and wellness.

Each section will provide tools, insights, and practices, merging science and intuition, so that readers can integrate somatic therapy into their lives with ease and impact. Below, I offer a glimpse into why I've chosen these topics and what each section will cover.

Section 1. Healing: The Foundation of Embodiment

Why Healing Matters:

What does it truly mean to heal? It's not just about removing pain—it's about reclaiming a sense of safety, regulation, and connection with yourself. It is about becoming whole again—feeling safe in your body, regulated in your nervous system, and grounded in your sense of self. Somatic therapy teaches that healing is not linear but cyclical, a return to yourself over and over again through presence and compassion.

What This Section Will Cover:

a. Understanding trauma from a somatic perspective: How the body stores unresolved experiences.

b. The role of the nervous system in healing, focusing on the interplay between the sympathetic and parasympathetic systems.

c. How emotional regulation begins in the body, not just the mind.

d. Healing as a process: Learning to navigate relapses, breakthroughs, and plateaus.

e. Stories from the field: Case studies that illustrate somatic healing in action.

Section 2. Toolbox: Building Personalized Practices

Why a Toolbox is Essential:

Each person's journey to embodiment is unique. What works for one individual may not resonate with another. A somatic toolbox ensures that clients and practitioners have a range of strategies to meet their ever-changing needs. This section provides practical, diverse techniques that can be tailored to suit different experiences and body-mind states.

What This Section Will Cover:

a. Key takeaway points summarizing the core concepts of somatic therapy.

b. A daily planner: Techniques spread out over 4 weeks to reconnect with the body for emotional regulation.

c. Journaling prompts for relaxation, energy, and focus.

d. An astrocartography guide: to use astrology and your birth chart for a more holistic somatic treatment.

Section 3. Exercises: The Language of Movement

Why Exercises Are Vital in Somatic Therapy:

Our bodies communicate through movement. Somatic exercises offer more than just physical activity—they help unlock emotions, integrate experiences, and promote deeper healing. This section focuses on movement practices that invite curiosity, self-compassion, and release, reconnecting readers to the wisdom of their bodies.

What This Section Will Cover:

a. Gentle, embodied movement exercises: Releasing tension, enhancing presence.

b. Trauma-informed movement practices: Creating safety and trust in the body.

c. Partner exercises to foster connection and co-regulation.

d. Micro-movements and body scanning as tools for cultivating mindfulness.

e. Movement as a metaphor: Exploring what our postures and patterns tell us about our emotional landscape.

Section 4. Coping Skills: Navigating Daily Life with Somatic Awareness

Why Coping Skills Are a Lifeline:

We cannot avoid stress or pain, but we can learn to meet them with tools that foster resilience. Somatic coping skills help us manage life's inevitable challenges with grace, tapping into the body's natural capacity to regulate and recover. This section will focus on actionable strategies that can be used in real time to promote well-being.

What This Section Will Cover:

a. Learning to ride the waves: Techniques for managing emotional highs and lows.

b. Somatic responses to anxiety, depression, and trauma triggers.

c. Self-soothing techniques: Calming the body and quieting the mind.

d. Developing boundaries and body autonomy as coping mechanisms.

e. How to cultivate resilience and post-traumatic growth through somatic practices.

Section 5. Yoga: Bridging Body, Mind, and Spirit

Why Yoga is Included:

Yoga is one of the most ancient, embodied practices we have—rooted in the understanding that healing happens when the body, mind, and spirit align. In this book, yoga will be explored through a somatic lens, not as an exercise routine but as a path to embodied awareness. Yoga can be a deeply transformative practice, inviting wholeness, stillness, and growth.

What This Section Will Cover:

a. Somatic yoga: Moving beyond postures into embodied presence.

b. Breath and movement synchronization: Regulating the nervous system through mindful flow.

c. Trauma-sensitive yoga practices: How to modify poses to create safety and accessibility.

d. Yoga nidra and body scans as tools for deep relaxation and integration.

e. The philosophy of yoga: Connecting the spiritual essence of yoga with somatic healing.

These five topics—Healing, Toolbox, Exercises, Coping Skills, and Yoga—create a framework that honors the complexity and beauty of somatic therapy. Each section offers practical tools, grounded wisdom, and heartfelt guidance to support your healing journey. The aim of this book is to empower people to come home to their bodies, trust their sensations, and use these five pillars as companions in their healing journey.

I hope that through these topics, readers will feel not only informed but transformed. Healing is not an end destination—it is an ongoing, embodied practice. This book is your guide to walking that path—step by step, breath by breath, movement by movement—until healing becomes a way of being.

BOOK 1

Healing

CHAPTER 1
WORKING WITH TRAUMA & PTSD IN THE BODY

When Ava first walked into my office, I could sense the weight she carried—both emotionally and physically. She moved cautiously, her shoulders curled inward, her steps tentative, as if her body was bracing itself against the world. After struggling with talk therapy, Ava's psychiatrist referred her to me, hoping a different approach could help.

At 36, she was experiencing debilitating symptoms of PTSD: insomnia, flashbacks, and a constant sense of dread. But what concerned her the most was the way her body seemed to betray her—her muscles were tight, her chest felt heavy, and she had frequent panic attacks that left her gasping for air. "I feel like I've tried everything," she told me during our first session, her voice trembling. "But my body won't stop. It's like I can't breathe fully."

My first step is always to listen to the body's history. Instead of rushing to dive into her trauma narrative, I took time to slowly understand her history—both through words and her body's responses. Ava grew up in an unstable environment with emotional neglect, compounded by an abusive relationship in her twenties. But it wasn't just what had happened to her that mattered; it was how her body held those experiences.

When she spoke about her trauma, her body would tense—her hands clenched into fists, her jaw tightened, and she unconsciously crossed her arms. I paid close attention to these cues. Trauma isn't just a memory—it's something the body carries, often long after the mind has tried to move on. We talked about her triggers—loud noises, crowded spaces—and how, in those moments, she would freeze or dissociate.

"It feels like I'm trapped in my own skin," Ava whispered, gripping the arms of the chair as if steadying herself. Ava said. "I can't make it stop."

My second step was to create safety and stabilization. Trauma survivors often lack a sense of safety within their own bodies. So, before we could begin releasing her trauma, we focused on stabilizing Ava's nervous system. I shared with Ava how the fight-flight-freeze response can become trapped in the body when trauma remains unresolved. My goal was to help her find ways to feel safe in her body again.

We started with grounding exercises—simple yet powerful practices like placing her feet firmly on the ground and becoming aware of how her body felt supported by the chair. Each session, we would begin by orienting to the present moment: I asked her to notice three things she could see, two things she could hear, and one thing she could feel. At first, these grounding exercises felt foreign to Ava. But with each session, I watched as she slowly reconnected with her body, finding small moments of safety in the present. These practices helped her develop a sense of being anchored in the here and now.

Ava told me, "For the first time in a long time, I feel like I have a little bit of control. Just being able to breathe and look around makes a difference."

The third step I took was to track the felt sense and release tension. As Ava became more comfortable with her body, we started working with what Peter Levine, the founder of Somatic Experiencing, calls the "felt sense"—the internal sensations that arise in the body. Each time she described her triggers or distress, I gently guided her to track where those sensations showed up in her body.

For example, when she talked about feeling overwhelmed, she noticed a knot in her stomach. I encouraged her to stay with that sensation, without trying to change or fix it, and simply allow it to unfold. At first, she found this difficult—her mind wanted to flee from discomfort. But over time, Ava learned to approach her sensations with curiosity. "It's like I can watch it instead of being overwhelmed by it," she observed.

In one particularly powerful session, Ava noticed a heavy, constricting feeling in her chest that she had felt during panic attacks. As she tracked the sensation, it began to shift—it moved down into her abdomen, then dissolved into a feeling of warmth. Afterward, she cried softly and said, "I think that was the fear I've been carrying for years." The body had finally released what words alone couldn't reach.

The fourth step was to integrate movement and boundaries. Somatic therapy isn't just about what happens on the mat or in the therapy room—it's about integrating those experiences into everyday life. I introduced movement exercises to help Ava rebuild a sense of agency and ownership over her body.

We practiced simple boundary-setting exercises. One exercise involved her standing still and extending her arms outward, imagining her personal space as a protective bubble. Another involved gentle, rhythmic movements—rolling her shoulders, swaying her hips—allowing her to feel free in her body. These movements were small but significant. More importantly, they became part of her daily life.

"A few weeks ago, I would've felt silly doing this," Ava admitted, shaking her head. "But now... I actually feel good. Like my body belongs to me again."

She began to use these tools in real life. For example, when she felt overwhelmed in public spaces, she would gently sway or roll her shoulders to regulate her nervous system. Slowly, her panic attacks decreased in frequency, and she began sleeping through the night without medication.

The fifth step is to fully embody healing and reclaiming your future. After six months of somatic work, Ava was a different person. She stood taller, her shoulders relaxed, her breath steady. She no longer lived in fear of her body's responses. "It's not that I'll never feel anxious again," she said during one of our final sessions. "But now, I know how to be with those feelings. I don't have to run from them anymore."

We spent our last few sessions reflecting on her journey and celebrating her progress. Trauma is never completely erased, but Ava now embodied a sense of resilience and self-trust that she hadn't thought possible. She expressed gratitude not only for the therapy but for her own body—for the way it had carried her through years of survival and now, finally, into healing.

"Somatic therapy gave me something no other therapy could," Ava told me. "It gave me myself back."

Ava's story is just one example of how trauma lives in the body. But what does this actually look like for others? Trauma can manifest physically in many different ways, often appearing as pain, tension, or chronic illness—sometimes even when there's no clear medical cause.

Ava's journey captures the essence of somatic therapy: Healing isn't about reliving the past or forcing change—it's about listening to the body and allowing it to release what it no longer needs. Trauma locks us into patterns of tension and fear, but the body also holds the key to freedom.

With each session, as Ava's breath deepened and her muscles softened, her nervous system learned to trust again. And with that trust came profound healing—not just the absence of symptoms but the presence of vitality and joy. Ava's story reminds me that somatic therapy is more than just a technique; it's an invitation to come home to ourselves, breath by breath, step by step.

In every client I work with, I see a reflection of this truth: The body remembers—but it also knows how to heal. Ava's story is just one example of how trauma lives in the body. But what does this actually look like for others? Trauma can manifest physically in many different ways, often appearing as pain, tension, or chronic illness—sometimes even when there's no clear medical cause.

How Trauma Manifests Somatically

Trauma profoundly affects both the mind and body. When you experience trauma, your body often holds onto the sensations and emotional responses linked to that event. This is known as somatic memory, where your body stores feelings, sensations, and reactions to traumatic experiences. Understanding how trauma manifests somatically is vital for effective healing.

Because trauma is stored in the body, it often manifests as chronic pain or unexplained physical symptoms. Here are some of them.

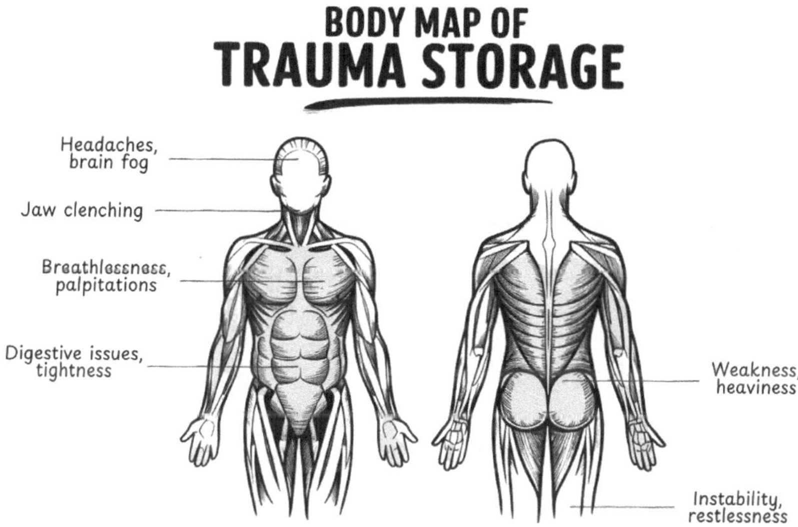

Symptom 1. Chronic Pain

Do you often experience persistent pain without a clear cause? This may be a manifestation of trauma. Here are some common examples:

Back Pain: Persistent back pain can make it difficult to sit or stand for long periods, often without a clear physical cause.

Headaches or Migraines: Frequent headaches can become debilitating and interfere with daily activities.

Joint Pain: Discomfort in areas like your knees or shoulders can make movement challenging.

Abdominal Pain: Conditions like irritable bowel syndrome can be linked to emotional distress.

Symptom 2. Muscle Tension

Frequently tightness or stiffness in your muscles could also be a result of trauma. Consider these manifestations:

Neck and Shoulder Tension: Discomfort in these areas can contribute to frequent headaches.

Jaw Clenching: This can lead to teeth grinding, especially at night.

Chest Tightness: You might experience difficulty breathing or a persistent sense of pressure in your chest.

Symptom 3. Fatigue

Feeling drained or lacking energy is a common response to trauma. Here are some signs to look out for:

Difficulty Waking Up: Struggling to wake up, even after a full night's sleep, can be a sign of trauma-related fatigue.

Low Energy Levels: Daily activities may feel exhausting or overwhelming.

Mental Drain: You may find it hard to concentrate or feel mentally exhausted, even after resting.

Symptom 4. Numbness or Disconnection

Feeling detached from your body or emotions is a common trauma response. This may manifest in the following ways:

Dissociation: You may feel as if you're watching yourself from the outside during stressful moments.

Lack of Physical Sensation: You might not feel pain or temperature changes as you normally would.

Difficulty Identifying Emotions: Recognizing or expressing your feelings can be challenging.

Symptom 5. Heightened States of Arousal

Do you often feel overly alert or on edge? This heightened state can result from trauma. Here are some examples:

Increased Heart Rate: You might notice your heart racing unexpectedly, even while sitting still or doing routine tasks.

Rapid Breathing: Shortness of breath may occur suddenly, even in moments of calm.

Excessive Sweating: You may find yourself sweating more than usual, even in non-stressful environments.

Symptom 6. Challenges in Feeling Safe and Grounded

Do you often feel unstable or insecure in your environment? Do you experience ongoing anxiety or distress? Here are some ways trauma can manifest in your sense of safety:

Avoiding Social Situations: You may steer clear of gatherings due to heightened anxiety.

Persistent Feelings of Dread: A constant sense that something bad will happen can leave you feeling uneasy.

Struggling with Routine Activities: Even simple daily tasks may feel overwhelming, leading to a desire to avoid them altogether.

These symptoms can disrupt your life, making it crucial to seek support and engage in practices that help reconnect your body and emotions.

Working Through Trauma

To begin working through trauma, you can engage in somatic practices. These techniques guide you to reconnect with your body, tuning into the sensations it holds. You can start by tuning into your physical sensations. This can help you understand the connections between your emotional experiences and bodily reactions.

Mindfulness is a powerful ally in your healing journey. It encourages you to focus on the present moment, acknowledging your thoughts and feelings without judgment. This practice helps cultivate awareness of bodily sensations. As you become more attuned to your body, you can recognize patterns associated with trauma.

Breathwork is an effective tool for processing trauma. By focusing on your breath, you can regulate your emotions and promote relaxation. Breath awareness creates a sense of safety within your body, allowing you to explore difficult emotions and facilitating emotional release.

You can incorporate grounding exercises to enhance your sense of safety. Grounding techniques, such as feeling your feet on the ground or noticing the weight of your body, can help you reconnect with the present moment. These practices remind you that you are in control and safe.

Ultimately, working with trauma in the body involves reconnecting with yourself. Acknowledging and addressing the somatic aspects of your experiences allows you to pave the way for healing and transformation. By understanding how trauma manifests physically, you can take proactive steps toward reclaiming your body and emotions.

Understanding Body Memory and Somatic Markers

Body memory refers to how your body retains and expresses emotional experiences, even if your mind doesn't consciously recall them. Even if your mind does not consciously recall them, your body still holds onto these memories. This concept suggests that your physical self can store memories related to emotional experiences. These memories often manifest as physical sensations, tensions, or movements. These stored memories influence your behavior, reactions, and overall well-being, and by working with them, somatic therapy helps you heal. This highlights the significance of somatic experiences in the therapeutic process.

Somatic markers are physical sensations, like tightness in the chest or a fluttering in the stomach, that arise when you're faced with emotional stimuli. This term was coined by neuroscientist Antonio Damasio. It emphasizes how your body uses these markers as indicators of emotional experiences. For instance, you might feel a tightening in your chest or a flutter in your stomach when faced with a stressful situation. These sensations serve as reminders of past experiences associated with similar emotions. They can guide your decision-making and responses in the moment.

Your body stores emotional experiences through various mechanisms. During intense emotional moments, your body undergoes physiological changes. These changes may include an increased heart rate, muscle tension, or altered breathing patterns. Your body reacts to intense emotions—tightening, speeding up, or altering its rhythm—and these reactions become imprinted, making it harder to forget the emotional experience. Later, when faced with similar emotions, your body may react without thinking, evoking the same sensations that were tied to the original experience.

Somatic therapy leverages body memory and somatic markers to facilitate healing. By focusing on bodily sensations, therapists encourage you to explore these physical responses. This process helps you connect with your emotional history. It often involves guided somatic awareness exercises. During these exercises, you are encouraged to identify and articulate your sensations. Through this exploration, you can gain insights into your emotional experiences. This understanding allows for deeper processing and healing.

Recognizing body memory and somatic markers underscores the importance of addressing the physical aspects of emotional experiences in therapy. Understanding how your body retains and expresses emotions allows you to approach healing in a more integrated way. This approach acknowledges the vital connection between your physical and emotional selves.

Integrating body memory and somatic markers into your healing process can be transformative, opening new pathways for emotional awareness and growth. You may discover that acknowledging physical sensations can lead to deeper emotional awareness. For example, noticing tension in your shoulders may signal stress or anxiety from a past experience. Exploring these sensations allows you to uncover their origins and effects, helping you better understand your emotional landscape.

As you engage in somatic therapy, you may also learn to recognize patterns in your body's responses. This awareness helps you identify triggers and develop healthier, more effective coping strategies. For instance, if you notice your heart racing when discussing a specific topic, you can explore why that topic elicits such a reaction. Understanding the connection between your body and emotions empowers you to respond more effectively in future situations.

Addressing body memory in therapy also gives you the opportunity to release long-held emotions that your body has been carrying. You might find that physical expressions, such as movement or breathwork, help process emotions that have been trapped in your body. These practices can create a powerful sense of release, providing relief and allowing you to move forward with more emotional space. They create room for fresh emotional experiences, making space for healing to unfold in both body and mind.

CHAPTER 2
GROUNDING AND SELF-REGULATION TECHNIQUES

When Daniel first sat down in my office, I noticed his knee bouncing uncontrollably, as if his body were stuck in a loop of nervous energy. His hands fidgeted, twisting the edges of his sleeve, and he let out a long sigh before even saying a word. Daniel, a 44-year-old tech consultant, came to me because his anxiety was spiraling out of control.

"I feel like I'm always on edge," he admitted. "Even when there's no reason to be anxious, my mind is racing, and my body just can't calm down. I've tried mindfulness apps and therapy before, but nothing sticks. I can't relax—no matter what I do."

For Daniel, stress wasn't just a fleeting experience; it was his daily reality. He described mornings when his heart would race before he even got out of bed, afternoons spent feeling tense in meetings, and evenings where his mind refused to switch off, no matter how exhausted he was. He knew his stress was affecting his health. Insomnia, digestive issues, and a constant feeling of burnout were his daily companions. But what troubled him most was how disconnected he felt from himself. "It's like I'm not even in my body," he said. "I'm just...wired."

The first step was understanding the patterns of dysregulation in Daniel's nervous system. The first step in our work together was to identify the ways his nervous system was dysregulated. Daniel was stuck in what's called a sympathetic state—a chronic fight-or-flight response where his body was constantly on alert, anticipating danger. This constant state wasn't helping him, but his body didn't know how to break free from it. I explained how somatic therapy helps the nervous system regulate itself, guiding the body to shift gently between moments of tension and relaxation.

The fight-or-flight response begins when a threat is perceived, activating the amygdala and hypothalamus in the brain. This triggers the adrenal glands to release adrenaline and cortisol, preparing the body for action. Physiological changes follow, including increased heart rate and heavy breathing. The body then takes fight-or-flight action to confront or escape the threat. Once the danger has passed, the recovery phase helps the body return to a balanced state.

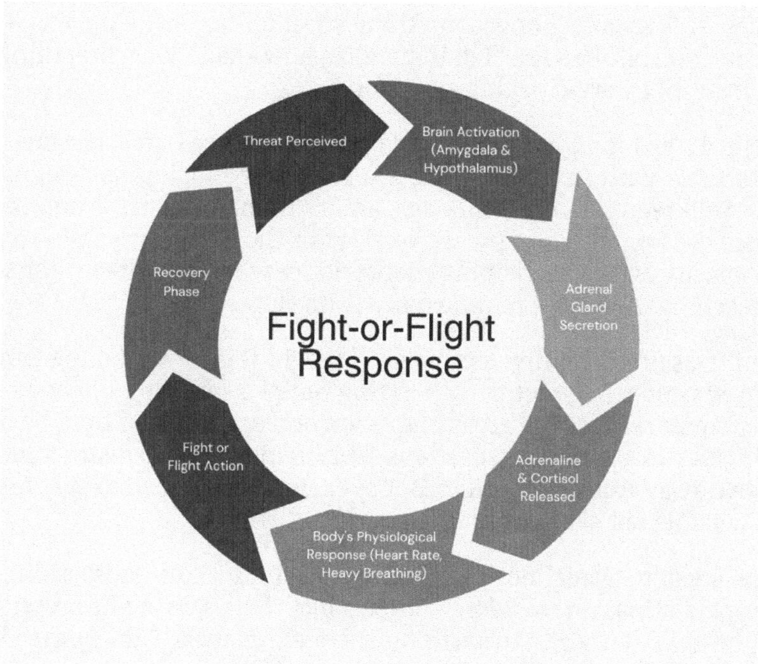

Through careful questioning and observation, I discovered that Daniel had spent years ignoring the signals from his body. "I've always powered through stress," he admitted. "I thought that's just how life was meant to be." Like many people, Daniel's strategy for dealing with discomfort had been to suppress it, but his body had reached its limit. Now, his system was locked in overdrive, unable to switch off.

The second step is establishing grounding practices. To help Daniel reconnect with his body and begin shifting out of this chronic state of tension, we started with grounding techniques. Grounding practices are simple yet transformative tools that anchor the mind and body in the present moment, allowing you to reclaim a sense of control. In our first few sessions, I introduced several techniques to see which ones resonated with him.

One of the practices that worked well for Daniel was orienting. I asked him to slowly look around the room, noticing the details of his environment—the colors, textures, sounds, and objects. "Notice three things you can see, two things you can hear, and one thing you can feel," I guided. This simple practice helped Daniel's nervous system recognize that he was safe in the moment, gently pulling him out of his anxious thoughts and back into his body.

Another grounding practice that Daniel found helpful was breath counting. Whenever his thoughts began to race, Daniel would close his eyes, place his hand on his belly, and focus on counting his inhales and exhales. "It's amazing how something so small can make me feel a little more in control," he said. "I didn't realize how shallow my breathing had become until I started paying attention."

The third step is building self-regulation skills. Once Daniel became more comfortable with grounding, we shifted to developing self-regulation skills. Self-regulation is the body's ability to manage stress and restore balance. In somatic therapy, we work with the nervous system to build this capacity over time, helping clients notice when they are dysregulated and teaching them how to return to a calm state.

One of the self-regulation techniques I taught Daniel was body scanning. In our sessions, he practic ed sitting quietly, scanning his body from head to toe, and noticing areas of tension or discomfort. At first, he found it difficult to sit with his sensations—his instinct was to distract himself or move away from discomfort. But over time, he learned to stay present with what he felt, without judgment.

In one session, Daniel noticed that his chest felt tight—something he'd never paid attention to before. "It feels like there's a weight pressing on me," he said. Rather than pushing the feeling away, I encouraged him to stay present with it, breathing into the sensation and observing what happened next. As he did, the tightness gradually softened. "It's strange," he said. "I always thought I needed to fight these feelings. But just being with them seems to help them loosen."

Another practice we used was rhythmic movement. I asked Daniel to try small, repetitive movements—like rocking gently forward and back while seated or swaying side to side. These movements mimic the body's natural self-soothing rhythm, much like how infants rock themselves to sleep. Daniel found these exercises especially helpful during moments of overwhelm. "When I sway, it feels like my body knows what to do," he said. "It's calming in a way I didn't expect."

The fourth step is integrating practices into daily life. These movements mimic the body's natural self-soothing rhythm, much like how infants rock themselves to sleep. I encouraged Daniel to use grounding and self-regulation techniques throughout his day—especially during stressful situations. For example, before important meetings, he would take a few moments to orient himself to the room, notice his breath, and consciously relax his shoulders.

Daniel also began using these practices during his commute, which had previously been a source of stress. Instead of scrolling through his phone to distract himself on the crowded subway, Daniel practiced breath counting and gentle body scanning. These small shifts helped him arrive at work feeling more centered and less reactive.

The fifth step is the transformation and long-term resilience. Instead of scrolling through his phone to distract himself on the crowded subway, Daniel practiced breath counting and gentle body scanning. His panic attacks became infrequent, and he noticed that he was able to manage stressful moments without feeling overwhelmed. "It's like my body finally knows how to settle," he told me. "I don't feel like I'm constantly bracing for impact anymore."

One of the most significant changes Daniel experienced was a sense of reconnection with himself. I used to feel like a head walking around, disconnected from everything below my neck," Daniel said, his voice softening. "Now, I actually feel my body. I can sense when I'm getting tense, and I know how to calm myself down."

In our final sessions, we discussed how he could continue using these tools in his everyday life. Daniel expressed gratitude not just for the techniques but for the shift in his mindset. "I thought I needed to control everything," he said. "But what I really needed was to listen to my body and give it what it needed."

Daniel's journey shows how grounding and self-regulation techniques can transform not just how we react to stress, but how we reconnect with ourselves. Anxiety often arises when the body is disconnected from the present moment, stuck in a loop of worry and tension. Grounding helps bring clients back to the here and now, while self-regulation builds the capacity to manage stress and restore balance.

Through our work together, Daniel learned to trust his body's ability to calm itself. This trust is the foundation of resilience—the knowledge that, no matter what life throws at you, your body has the tools to find its way back to equilibrium. Daniel's story is a reminder that healing doesn't always require grand gestures. Sometimes, it's the smallest practices—breathing, swaying, noticing—that create the deepest change.

And in those small moments, healing becomes a way of life.

The Importance of Grounding Techniques

Grounding is a technique that helps you feel more connected to the present moment and your surroundings. It can reduce feelings of anxiety, stress, or disconnection. Grounding techniques often involve tuning into your senses—what you can see, hear, feel, smell, or even taste.

Deep breathing is another effective grounding method. You can also try physical activities, like walking or stretching, to reconnect with your body. Grounding helps you feel stable and secure, making it easier to navigate overwhelming emotions and regain control over racing thoughts. It's a useful tool for calming the mind and body.

Grounding techniques serve as a lifeline, pulling you back into your body and your surroundings. Understanding their importance is vital for overall mental well-being.

Connecting to the Present

In today's fast-paced world, it's easy to get caught up in worries about the past or anxieties about the future. Anxiety often arises from worrying about what might happen next. Grounding techniques gently pull your focus back to the present moment, helping you reconnect with the here and now. By anchoring yourself in the present, you can break free from the grip of anxiety and panic, finding peace in the moment. You learn to appreciate the moment, leading to a greater sense of calm.

Enhancing Self-Awareness

Grounding helps you become more aware of your body and emotions. Grounding helps you become attuned to your body's signals—recognizing when tension builds or when emotions begin to rise. This awareness empowers you to respond before anxiety takes control. This heightened awareness is crucial for emotional regulation. You can identify when you are feeling anxious or overwhelmed. With this knowledge, you can employ grounding techniques before your feelings escalate.

Reducing Anxiety and Stress

Anxiety can feel like a heavy weight on your chest. It can make it hard to breathe and think clearly. Grounding techniques provide immediate relief. They help you shift your focus away from racing thoughts. Simple techniques like deep breathing or feeling your feet on the ground can calm your nervous system. As you ground yourself, your heart rate steadies, and the tightness in your body begins to release, leaving you calmer and more centered. This physiological response reduces feelings of stress and anxiety.

Techniques for Sensory Awareness

Technique 1. *Five Senses Exercise*

This simple exercise is a great way to help you reconnect with your senses. Follow these steps:

a. See: Identify five things you can see. Look for details in your environment, like colors, shapes, and textures.

b. Touch: Tune into four things you can touch, feeling the texture of your clothes, the surface of a table, or the sensation of your feet on the ground.

Hold an object and focus on its texture.

c. Hear: Listen for three sounds. Focus on background noises, like birds chirping or the hum of a fan.

d. Smell: Notice two scents—perhaps the fragrance of food, fresh air after rain, or even the smell of your environment.

Taste: Notice one taste. If you have something to eat or drink, savor the flavors. If not, recall a favorite taste in your mind.

Technique 2. *Grounding with Nature*

Spending time in nature connects you more deeply to your senses and the world around you. Go for a walk in a park or garden. Notice the sights, sounds, and smells around you. Nature engages all your senses, helping you feel more grounded and connected to the earth.

Technique 3. *Mindful Eating*

Mindful eating is a powerful way to heighten sensory awareness, allowing you to slow down and truly connect with the food you're enjoying. Choose a small piece of food, such as a raisin or a slice of fruit. Before eating, observe its color, shape, and texture. As you eat, pay attention to the flavors, textures, and sensations as you eat, savoring each bite fully. Chew slowly and savor each bite. This practice allows you to reconnect with your sense of taste, fostering mindfulness and gratitude for the nourishment your food provides.

Technique 4. *Guided Imagery*

Guided imagery uses your imagination to create a sensory experience. Close your eyes and imagine yourself in a peaceful place, like a beach or a forest. Visualize the sights, sounds, and smells around you, letting them come alive in your mind. Picture the details: the sound of waves, the scent of pine, or the warmth of the sun on your skin. This technique helps you engage your senses and promotes relaxation.

Technique 5. *Breath and Body Awareness*

Combining breath awareness with sensory practices deepens your experience. Sit or lie comfortably. As you breathe, pay attention to how your body feels—where it's tense, where it's relaxed, and how the rhythm of your breath grounds you. Feel the rise and fall of your chest. Acknowledge any areas of tension or relaxation. This practice cultivates a greater awareness of your physical sensations.

CHAPTER 3
BREATH AS A HEALING TOOL

As a somatic therapist, I've spent years guiding clients through their healing journeys. But there was a point when my own body demanded that I listen. It happened three years ago, after the pandemic had pushed my private practice into a virtual format. The transition brought an unexpected wave of stress. On the outside, I appeared to be managing—seeing clients from my apartment and offering grounding techniques and breathwork over Zoom.

I didn't notice the signs at first—just a nagging tightness in my chest and shallow breathing that I brushed off as "normal stress." Then came the restless nights, where my mind spun endlessly through a maze of to-do lists and worries. One afternoon, as I sat down to respond to emails, a wave of panic hit me out of nowhere—my heart raced, and a feeling of suffocation washed over me. My heart raced, my chest tightened, and it felt like the walls of my apartment were closing in. I recognized this feeling all too well—anxiety, creeping in like an old, familiar shadow, suffocating and relentless. And for the first time in years, I realized that I was the one in need of the practices I taught others.

I knew I had to slow down, take a moment, and listen to my body before it became too much to bear. In somatic therapy, the breath is often the first tool we use when we feel overwhelmed. It's a simple yet profound anchor, bringing us back to ourselves. Not because it's a cure-all, but because it connects us to life—moment by moment, inhale by exhale. And so, I sat cross-legged on my yoga mat, placed one hand on my heart and the other on my belly, and simply began to notice my breath.

At first, my breath was shallow, trapped high in my chest—tight and constricted, a clear sign that my nervous system was stuck in fight-or-flight. I didn't try to force my breath deeper. In somatic therapy, we're taught to honor the body's rhythm, to allow instead of forcing. So, I just observed—breath in, breath out—and tried to soften around the tightness.

As the minutes passed, I gently elongated my exhalations, following the principle that longer exhales activate the parasympathetic nervous system—our body's natural response to calm and restore. I inhaled for a count of four and exhaled for six. Slowly, I felt my body respond. My heartbeat steadied, my shoulders dropped, and the tightness in my chest began to dissolve, little by little.

The breath opened a doorway for me to feel what was going on beneath the anxiety. With my eyes closed, I tracked the sensations that rose to the surface—a knot in my stomach, a heaviness in my throat, a dull ache behind my eyes. I resisted the urge to label or fix them. Instead, I allowed them to be, breathing into the discomfort with patience and acceptance. Instead, I used my breath to stay with the sensations, riding them like waves.

This process of tracking sensations—something I had done with clients so many times—was humbling to experience firsthand. Some sensations came and went quickly, while others lingered. I noticed that when I exhaled slowly, the knot in my stomach softened. With each breath, I wasn't just calming my body—I was offering it presence.

After about 20 minutes of breathwork, I let my body settle into stillness. A deep sense of relief washed over me, as if I had been carrying tension I hadn't even noticed. I placed both hands on my belly and let my breath flow naturally, without counting or controlling it.

A wave of emotion surfaced—grief, fatigue, and frustration I hadn't allowed myself to fully feel. Tears welled up, and I let them come. In somatic therapy, we understand that emotions are simply energy in motion—if we allow them to flow, they move through us instead of becoming trapped. I stayed with the tears, breathing through them, fully present with the emotion, until they slowly subsided.

When the emotion passed, I felt a deep lightness, like a weight had been lifted from my body. My breath had become deeper and smoother, moving freely into my belly. And with that freedom came a quiet sense of peace—a reminder that I didn't need to fix anything. I just needed to be present with what was already there.

Over the following weeks, I made breathwork a daily ritual. Each morning, before starting my day, I took ten minutes to sit with my breath—nothing fancy, just slow, mindful breathing with a hand on my heart. It became my anchor, a way to check in with my body before the demands of the day pulled me in different directions.

There were still moments of overwhelm—emails piling up, clients in crisis, life unfolding with its usual unpredictability. But I noticed that I responded differently. When my chest tightened or my thoughts began to race, I would pause, place my hand on my belly, and take a few slow breaths. My body learned that it was safe to relax, even amidst the chaos, by simply returning to my breath.

That experience reminded me of a profound truth: even those of us who guide others need to come back to our own bodies. Healing is not a destination; it is a practice—a daily invitation to listen, breathe, and be with whatever arises.

Breath, in somatic therapy, is more than just something we do—it's a gateway to healing, a bridge that reconnects us with the present moment. It is a bridge—a way to reconnect with the present moment, soothe the nervous system, and make space for emotions to flow. Through my breathwork practice, I found my way back to myself—not by escaping the stress, but by meeting it with compassion, curiosity, and a deep sense of presence.

That experience shifted the way I show up for my clients, too. I now emphasize to them—and to myself—that healing is about returning, again and again, to the breath. Whether it's in moments of panic or in the quiet spaces of the morning, the breath is always there, waiting to guide us home.

The role of breathing as a healing tool

Breath is the bridge between your mind and body, linking the mental and physical, grounding us in the present moment. When you focus on your breath, you can access and regulate your emotions. This connection is the gateway to profound healing, self-awareness, and emotional balance.

Breath has the power to influence your physiological state, shaping how you feel in your body and mind. When you are stressed, your breath becomes shallow and rapid, mirroring the tension and anxiety that builds up in your body. This activates the sympathetic nervous system, preparing you for a fight-or-flight response. Conversely, slow, deep breathing activates the parasympathetic nervous system, which is our natural calming response—slowing the heart rate, relaxing muscles, and easing the mind. This response promotes relaxation and calmness. Understanding this connection is key to using breathwork effectively.

In somatic therapy, we use breath to explore emotional states—gently guiding the body and mind back into balance. You can use your breath to uncover feelings stored in the body. For example, when you take deep breaths, you may notice sensations or emotions surfacing. This awareness allows you to process and release these feelings. It can bring clarity and understanding to your emotional landscape. These are some ways in which breathing helps:

Way 1. Regulates the Nervous System

Breathing helps shift your body from a fight-or-flight state into a rest-and-digest mode, calming the nervous system and promoting healing. Conscious, deep breathing calms the body, reduces anxiety, and supports emotional regulation.

Way 2. Increases Body Awareness (Interoception)

Focusing on the breath enhances interoception—the ability to sense internal bodily states. This heightened awareness helps clients reconnect with their bodies, notice sensations linked to stress or trauma, and respond more mindfully.

Way 3. Releases Tension and Trauma

Breathwork creates space for emotional release, as trauma often restricts breathing patterns (e.g., shallow or held breaths). By deepening the breath, clients gradually release tension stored in muscles and tissues, facilitating the body's natural healing process.

Making the most of breathing:

Somatic therapy is a holistic approach that connects the mind and body, facilitating healing and transformation. It offers several benefits across various systems in the body, including the respiratory system, nervous system, immune system, emotional regulation, physical tension, and energy levels. Here's an exploration of these transformative effects:

Effect 1. Practice Breath Awareness

Start by mindfully observing your natural breath, without trying to alter it. Notice where you feel the breath in your body—whether it's in your chest, belly, or nose—and observe how it subtly shifts as you experience different emotions or tension. This practice enhances your interoception, gently guiding you to reconnect with your body and its sensations.

Effect 2. Incorporate Deep, Diaphragmatic Breathing

Engage your diaphragm by breathing deeply into your belly, letting it expand with each inhale, rather than taking shallow breaths into your chest. Inhale deeply through your nose, letting your belly expand, then exhale slowly and fully through your mouth. This deep breathing activates the parasympathetic nervous system, helping you relax and regulate your emotions, bringing balance and calm.

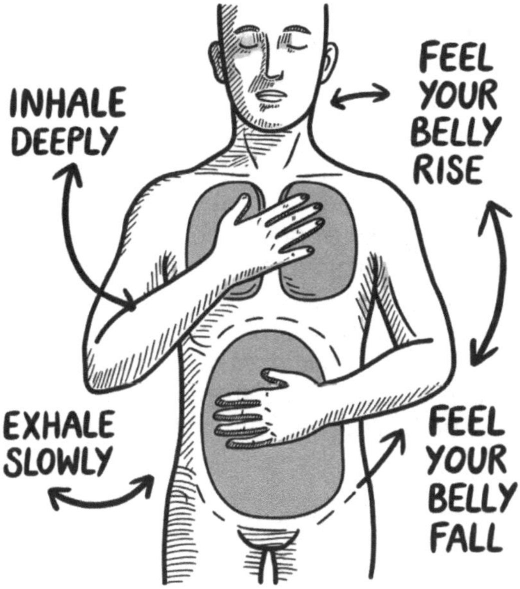

Effect 3. Use Rhythmic or Box Breathing for Grounding

Techniques like box breathing (inhale for 4 counts, hold for 4, exhale for 4, hold for 4) create a calming rhythm that stabilizes your nervous system, helping you stay grounded and prevent overwhelm. These structured breathing exercises are especially helpful in moments of anxiety or dysregulation, offering you a tool to center yourself and bring calm.

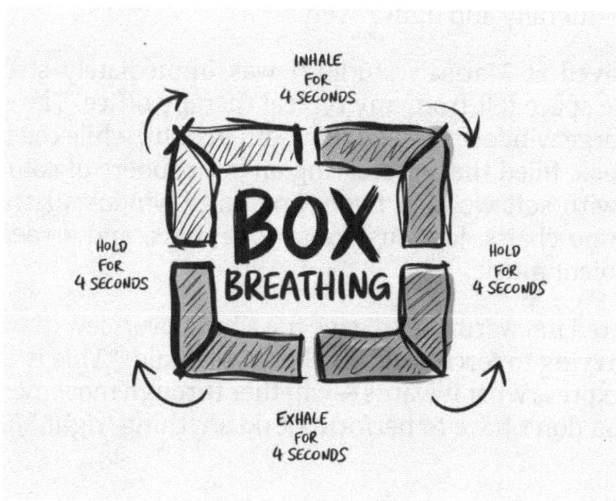

CHAPTER 4
MOVEMENT AND EXPRESSIVE PRACTICES

Even therapists need therapy. That's something I've always known, but it hit me hard last winter when life started feeling heavy in ways I couldn't explain. I was exhausted—not just the kind of tired that comes from overworking, but a bone-deep fatigue that made everything, even rest, feel like an insurmountable weight. My breathwork rituals weren't helping the way they usually did. My body felt stuck, tight, and unwilling to cooperate. I realized that I needed something different—something beyond the tools I had used for others. I needed to reconnect with my own body in a new way. I'd spent so much time guiding others through their somatic healing—maybe it was time to let someone else guide me.

That's how I found myself sitting across from Marisa, a somatic therapist in Brooklyn whose approach blended movement and expressive practices—a method I had never fully explored before. I'd heard of Marisa through mutual colleagues and decided to reach out. When I explained my situation—how I felt trapped in my own body despite all my tools—she gently suggested we try a movement session together. "Sometimes the body just needs a new way to speak," she said with a soft smile.

I agreed, though a part of me felt hesitant, as I was more accustomed to stillness than to movement. I was used to stillness—to sitting with sensations, tracking them, and gently breathing through discomfort. Movement, on the other hand, felt foreign. But I trusted Marisa and knew that if I was going to find a way out of this stuckness, I needed to move differently—literally and figuratively.

When I arrived at Marisa's studio, I was immediately struck by how different the space felt from any typical therapy office. The soft wooden floors and large windows bathed the room in light, while the faint hum of ambient music filled the air, creating an atmosphere of calm. The room was open, with soft wooden floors and large windows letting in light. There were no chairs, just cushions, yoga mats, and a speaker quietly playing ambient music.

Marisa greeted me warmly and gave me a brief overview of what we'd do. "We're not trying to force anything here," she said. "This is about letting your body express what it wants—whether through movement, sound, or stillness. You don't have to perform or do anything 'right.' Just see what shows up."

She began by guiding me through a grounding exercise—something familiar. We stood in place, feet planted firmly on the floor, and she asked me to notice the sensations in my body: the weight in my legs, the tension in my shoulders, and the tightness in my chest. I closed my eyes and took a deep breath, but even then, my body felt stiff and resistant—like it was unwilling to soften, unwilling to release the tension that had built up over time.

Then Marisa invited me to start with a small, rhythmic sway, just shifting my weight from side to side. At first, it felt awkward—my mind kept asking, "Am I doing this right?" But Marisa's voice was gentle, reassuring. "There's no right or wrong here," she said. "Just follow whatever feels good—or even what feels strange."

After a few minutes of swaying, something unexpected happened. As I tuned into the rhythm of my body, I noticed that my breath started to deepen—without effort. My arms, which had felt heavy and glued to my sides, slowly began to loosen, and an urge to stretch them wide spread through my body. It felt as if I was reaching for something beyond myself. Marisa noticed the shift. "Good," she said quietly. "Stay with that—what happens if you let your arms move however they want?"

I closed my eyes and let my arms begin to circle slowly, feeling the air brush against my skin. And then, without warning, my body took over—my hands clenched into fists, and my arms began to swing with an intensity I couldn't control. A surge of frustration and anger rose from deep within, pouring into my movement like a flood. I felt an unexpected surge of frustration rise up from my chest, spilling into my movement.

Marisa gave me permission to follow it. "If your body wants to express something, let it. Use sound if it helps."

I hadn't realized how much frustration I'd been carrying—weeks, maybe months, of bottled-up tension that my breathwork hadn't touched. I started moving more vigorously, swinging my arms, stomping my feet, and letting out small, guttural noises. The release felt cathartic—like I was wringing out the stress that had been lodged deep inside me.

Eventually, the intense movement slowed on its own, like a wave receding after crashing against the shore. I found myself on the floor, sitting cross-legged, my body trembling slightly but in a good way—like something inside me had finally shifted. Marisa sat beside me quietly, holding space.

"Just notice what's here now," she whispered. "There's no rush to explain or understand. Just feel it."

I placed my hand on my heart, feeling the steady thump beneath my palm. My breath was slow and full—deeper than it had been in weeks. For the first time in a long time, I felt a sense of lightness, like a knot inside me had unraveled.

Marisa gave me time to rest in that space before gently guiding me into an integration exercise. “Lie down if that feels good,” she suggested. “Let’s just let everything settle.”

I lay on the mat, arms and legs spread comfortably, and she invited me to scan my body one more time. This time, instead of tension, I felt warmth—a quiet, gentle hum of aliveness coursing through me.

Afterward, Marisa and I sat on the floor together, reflecting on what had just happened. “I think I was stuck in a loop,” I admitted. “I kept trying to breathe my way through the tension, but what I really needed was to move through it.”

Marisa nodded knowingly. “Sometimes the body doesn’t just want to settle—it wants to express. Movement lets the nervous system complete cycles that get stuck.” She paused and smiled. “It’s like finishing a sentence you didn’t know you’d started.”

That session with Marisa reminded me of the power of movement—how the body sometimes needs more than stillness and breath. It was humbling to be on the receiving end of somatic work, to experience firsthand how movement can unlock emotions that the mind can’t reach.

Over the next few weeks, I began incorporating more movement into my personal practice—not in a structured or performative way, but in small, intuitive moments. I found myself swaying while waiting for the subway, stretching my arms between sessions, and allowing my body to move when it needed to, instead of forcing it to be still.

There was a new sense of freedom in my body—a lightness I hadn’t felt in a long time. And with that freedom came a renewed sense of compassion for myself. I realized that healing isn’t always about calming down; sometimes, it’s about letting go through movement and expression.

That session with Marisa didn’t just help me release what I’d been holding—it reminded me that healing is an ongoing process, one that requires flexibility and curiosity. Breath is a powerful tool, but it’s not the only one. Sometimes, the body needs more—it needs to move, to express, to be free. Sometimes, the body needs to move in ways the mind struggles to comprehend, and that’s okay. And that’s okay.

That day in Marisa’s studio, I reconnected with a part of myself that had been buried—hidden beneath the weight of stress and expectations, waiting to be remembered. Movement became my way back to my body—a reminder that healing doesn’t always come through stillness, but sometimes through action, expression, and release. It comes, instead, in whatever form the body needs at the moment: a breath, a stretch, a stomp, or a dance.

As therapists, we often pour so much of ourselves into holding space for others that we forget to offer that same gift of care to ourselves. Marisa gave me that gift, and in doing so, she reminded me that even in my stuckness, my body knows the way forward. I just needed to trust it, to let it move freely.

Types of Movement Practices

Movement in somatic therapy can take many forms—from structured sequences grounded in ancient traditions to spontaneous, intuitive gestures that arise in the moment. Each type serves a unique purpose, allowing the body to express, release, and reconnect with the freedom and vitality it deserves. Below, we'll explore the different categories of movement practices used in somatic therapy and how they contribute to healing.

Category 1. Structured Movements

Structured movements are guided practices with defined forms, like yoga, Tai Chi, and Qigong.

Purpose: These practices offer predictable movements that foster stability, relaxation, and help you cultivate mindful awareness of your body.

Example: A simple yoga flow helps clients build strength and flexibility while also developing breath awareness and emotional regulation.

Who It Helps: Clients who find comfort in structure—those who feel overwhelmed by too much spontaneity—often benefit from these grounding rituals.

Category 2. Intuitive Movements

Intuitive movement allows the body to move freely without pre-planned patterns, following natural impulses as they arise—giving the body space to express itself without restraint.

Purpose: Intuitive movement promotes emotional release and liberation, allowing the body to express itself without the mind's need for control or judgment.

Example: Dancing alone to music with eyes closed, letting the body decide how it wants to move.

Who It Helps: This practice is especially helpful for individuals reconnecting with their bodies after trauma, offering a safe space to explore self-expression without judgment or fear.

Category 3. Micro-Movements

Small, subtle movements can unlock deep, lingering sensations, providing a way to gently reconnect with your body. These shifts are particularly useful when larger movements feel overwhelming.

Example: Slowly rolling the shoulders or shifting the neck from side to side.

Purpose: Micro-movements help clients re-establish body awareness, particularly in areas where chronic tension or numbness may have developed, offering a gentle approach to release.

Application: This technique is helpful for those working through trauma, as it allows for gentle engagement without overwhelming the nervous system.

Category 4. Rhythmic Movement

Rhythmic movements mirror natural motions like swaying, rocking, or walking, helping soothe the nervous system and bring a sense of calm. This practice profoundly impacts the body by mimicking self-soothing rhythms, like a parent gently rocking a baby back to calmness.

- Example: Gently swaying side to side while standing, or using repetitive foot tapping to release nervous energy.

- Purpose: Rhythm anchors you in the present moment, easing your body into relaxation and helping shift your nervous system out of fight-or-flight mode.

- Who It Helps: Especially helpful for individuals with anxiety or panic disorders, this practice uses repetition to foster a deep sense of safety and stability.

Category 5. Exploratory Movement

Exploratory movement invites you to follow prompts or cues to discover the patterns of tension, posture, or sensation your body holds, unlocking deeper awareness. It encourages curiosity and exploration over perfection, allowing you to make sense of your body's stories and experiences without judgment.

- Example: A therapist might ask, "What happens if you let your arms move in a way that expresses how you feel right now?"

- Purpose: This practice opens the door to new insights about how emotions and memories are stored in your body, helping you unlock layers of healing.

- Application: It's useful in sessions where words fall short, encouraging non-verbal exploration of emotions and physical sensations.

Category 6. Movement as a Metaphor for Emotional States

Movements often reflect inner emotional experiences. Hunched shoulders might indicate fear or withdrawal, while wide, expansive postures suggest openness and confidence. Therapists can invite clients to explore these body patterns metaphorically, shifting between postures and noticing emotional changes.

- Example: A client might move from a collapsed posture to a more upright stance and reflect on how that shift feels emotionally.

- Purpose: Using movement as a metaphor helps clients notice how emotions shape their physical form and teaches them how to embody new states of being.

- Who It Helps: Who It Helps: Especially effective for those working through shame, trauma, or emotional repression, this practice creates a safe, physical space for transformation and release.

By offering a variety of movement practices—from subtle micro-movements to expansive full-body exploration—somatic therapy meets you where you are, honoring your body's needs and pace. Movement allows your nervous system to shift, adapt, and release cycles of tension, creating room for new ways of being and expressing yourself in the world. Whether structured or freeform, these practices invite participants to explore their bodies as tools for self-discovery, healing, and expression.

CHAPTER 5
VISUALIZATION AND GUIDED IMAGERY

The principles of movement and somatic therapy are not just tools I use with clients—they have become essential to my own healing journey as well. Recently, I had the chance to help my mother, who was struggling with anxiety following a traumatic experience. My mother, a vibrant woman in her late 60s, had always been active, but after a fall in her apartment, something shifted in her. Even though she wasn't seriously injured, the experience left her frightened and emotionally shaken. She became unusually tense, unable to relax, and fearful of simple movements like climbing stairs or going for her evening walks.

Watching her withdraw into fear broke my heart. I could see the trauma settling into her body, creating a sense of paralysis. I knew that words alone wouldn't ease what she was feeling, so I decided to guide her through an experience using somatic principles—specifically visualization, guided imagery, and gentle movement.

We began our session seated comfortably in her cozy living room, the soft light filtering in through the windows, creating a calm and peaceful atmosphere. I explained that we would use visualization as a way to restore a sense of safety in her body. I asked her to close her eyes and imagine a place where she felt completely safe and peaceful. Without hesitation, she described a familiar image—her childhood garden in Queens, where she spent hours as a little girl surrounded by flowers and the gentle hum of bees.

As she described the garden, I invited her to explore it more deeply. "What colors do you see?" I asked. "What does the air feel like on your skin? Can you hear the birds?" I watched as the tension in her shoulders eased, and her breath began to deepen, flowing more freely. The stillness in the room seemed to shift. She was already starting to relax, her nervous system shifting into a calmer state.

Using guided imagery, I asked her to imagine herself standing barefoot on the garden's warm soil. "Feel the earth supporting your feet," I said. "Let your body remember what it feels like to be grounded and steady." This visualization helped her nervous system reconnect with a memory of safety and trust—something her body desperately needed after the fall.

Once I noticed her body softening and relaxing, I gently introduced movement—something small and simple to start. Trauma often leaves people stuck in a freeze response—the body feels immobile, even when no threat is present. I knew that getting my mother to move again, even in small ways, was essential.

I invited her to imagine herself walking through the vibrant garden of her childhood. “What if you took a step forward?” I asked. “Feel your feet touch the soft grass. Notice how it feels to take one gentle step after another.” She followed the imagery, and I noticed her body start to shift—her arms relaxed slightly, and she swayed, just a little, as if she were walking through that garden in real life.

I encouraged her to move in whatever way felt good. She began lifting her arms slowly, as if she were picking flowers from imaginary bushes. The movement was gentle, but it carried deep significance. It spoke to her nervous system, gently reminding her that it was safe to move, that she wasn’t trapped in the paralysis of fear anymore.

To close our session, I guided her into a seated position, inviting her to plant her feet firmly on the ground. She felt a deep sense of stability—grounded and at ease. We returned to the visualization one last time. “Picture yourself sitting in the garden now,” I said. “You’ve picked a bouquet of your favorite flowers. Feel the sun on your skin, the warmth in your body, and the ease in your breath.”

I placed my hand gently on her back, guiding her to take slow, deep breaths, imagining the sweet scent of flowers filling her lungs. “With every exhale, feel your body letting go of fear,” I whispered. “With every inhale, welcome in safety.”

After a few minutes, my mother opened her eyes, her face relaxed, and a sense of calm washed over her. “I didn’t realize how tense I’ve been,” she said quietly. It feels like the weight of the world has lifted,” she said softly, her voice tinged with relief.

That session wasn’t a quick fix, but it marked a turning point for my mother—a moment when she began to feel the shift. Over the next few days, she began taking small walks again, first around her apartment and later in the park. She told me that whenever fear started to creep in, she would close her eyes and return to the image of her childhood garden, feeling the warmth of the earth beneath her feet, grounding her in the moment.

Helping my mother through that moment reminded me of the transformative power of somatic therapy—not just as a tool for my clients, but as a deeply personal way to reconnect with the people I love. Visualization and movement allowed her body to release the fear that had taken hold after her fall, showing her that safety and freedom could be found again, one breath and step at a time.

This experience deepened my understanding of trauma recovery: Healing isn't about forcing movement; it's about inviting the body to feel safe enough to move again, to trust the process of release. It's about creating new pathways of trust and ease, even when the nervous system feels stuck. Sometimes, healing doesn't come from complex techniques; it comes from simple, gentle gestures—a walk through an imaginary garden, a hand on the back, a breath shared between mother and daughter.

Definition and Purpose of Visualization

Visualization is a transformative therapeutic tool that plays a key role in somatic therapy, guiding individuals toward healing and self-awareness. It involves creating mental images that evoke specific feelings or responses. This process fosters deep relaxation, emotional healing, and helps you reconnect with your innermost self. When you visualize, you harness the power of your imagination to create vivid mental images that evoke specific emotional responses. These images might be soothing landscapes, radiant healing energies, or even abstract representations of emotions, each offering a unique pathway to relaxation and release.

The purpose of visualization in somatic therapy is multifaceted. It can help you access buried emotions, create a sense of safety, and enhance your overall well-being. Visualization allows you to tap into the depths of your subconscious mind, unlocking a powerful avenue for deeper emotional healing and release. By envisioning calming or healing imagery, you invite relaxation into your body and mind, which can be especially effective in managing stress, anxiety, and overwhelming emotions.

Visualization acts as a bridge between your mind and body, helping you connect with the sensations and emotions within. Focusing on your mental imagery helps you reconnect with your bodily sensations, guiding you to become more attuned to your emotions and their physical manifestations. This connection can lead to increased self-awareness and a greater understanding of your emotional landscape.

The Science Behind Visualization and the Nervous System

Visualization and guided imagery are more than just mental exercises; they have measurable effects on the brain and body, offering powerful tools for healing. Somatic therapy leverages visualization to support emotional regulation, alleviate trauma, and foster resilience by actively engaging the nervous system. This section delves into the neuroscience behind visualization, focusing on neuroplasticity, the autonomic nervous system, and the role of mirror neurons. It demonstrates how mental imagery can rewire the brain and transform bodily responses.

Neuroplasticity: Rewiring the Brain through Visualization

Neuroplasticity is the brain's remarkable ability to reorganize itself, forming new neural connections in response to our experiences. This concept is at the heart of modern trauma recovery, offering a profound message of hope: the brain is not static—it has the power to heal, adapt, and transform, no matter where you are in life. Visualization plays a critical role in this process by helping the brain develop healthier responses to stress, pain, and trauma.

When we repeatedly imagine certain scenarios, movements, or emotional states, the brain processes these imagined experiences as though they were real. Research has shown that visualizing activities or emotions activates the same neural pathways involved in performing those actions or feeling those emotions. For example, studies show that mental practice—such as visualizing success—activates the same brain regions as actually performing the task, whether it's visualizing a perfect tennis serve or picturing yourself handling a stressful situation with calm. For trauma survivors, visualizing the completion of an unresolved survival response—such as running to safety—can help the nervous system 'finish' what was interrupted, allowing them to release trapped energy and reduce the lingering effects of trauma.

In somatic therapy, guided imagery helps the brain shift away from patterns of hypervigilance, fear, or avoidance. With time, these positive mental experiences create new neural pathways, promoting feelings of calm, safety, and relaxation. By engaging their imagination, clients can retrain their nervous systems, shifting to healthier, more adaptive responses when faced with stress or challenge.

Impact on the Autonomic Nervous System: Balancing Fight-or-Flight and Rest-and-Digest

The autonomic nervous system (ANS) is responsible for regulating involuntary functions, such as heart rate, digestion, and breathing. It plays a crucial role in how we respond to stress and regulate our internal state. The ANS is divided into two branches: the sympathetic nervous system (SNS), which activates the fight-or-flight response when we're under threat, and the parasympathetic nervous system (PNS), which helps us relax and recover after stress. Trauma, chronic stress, and emotional dysregulation can leave the nervous system stuck in an overactivated fight-or-flight state. This state keeps individuals trapped in anxiety, hypervigilance, or emotional numbness, preventing them from fully processing or relaxing.

Visualization and guided imagery can directly influence the balance between the SNS and PNS, helping the body move from a heightened, stress-driven state to a place of deep relaxation and calm. For example, simply imagining a peaceful, safe environment can activate the PNS, slowing the heart rate, deepening the breath, and enveloping the body in a sense of calm and safety. Visualizing warm light or soothing sensations moving through the body can reduce muscle tension and ease symptoms like a racing heart or shallow breathing.

In trauma recovery, visualization plays a vital role in helping to regulate the nervous system by introducing cues of safety that allow the body to feel secure once again, even when external circumstances may not immediately feel safe. Many trauma survivors struggle to feel safe even in non-threatening environments because their nervous system remains locked in survival mode. By consistently visualizing calming images or engaging in gentle movements, clients retrain their nervous system to activate the parasympathetic response more easily. Over time, this practice builds emotional resilience, helping them navigate life's challenges with greater ease.

Mirror Neurons: The Brain Responds to Imagined Experience as Real

One of the most intriguing discoveries in neuroscience is the role of mirror neurons—specialized brain cells that fire both when we perform an action and when we observe or even imagine someone else performing the same action. These neurons enable the brain to treat imagined experiences as if they were real, making visualization a profoundly transformative tool for healing and change.

In somatic therapy, mirror neurons help clients access bodily sensations and movements that may feel too overwhelming or painful to perform physically, allowing them to heal at their own pace. For example, a client recovering from physical injury or trauma may visualize themselves moving freely and comfortably—and the brain will respond as if the body is truly engaging in that movement. This can be profoundly healing, especially for individuals who feel disconnected from their bodies or fearful of certain actions.

Mirror neurons also play a pivotal role in empathy and emotional healing, helping us reconnect with feelings of care, comfort, and compassion. When clients visualize being held or comforted, their brains activate emotional circuits linked to the experience of receiving care and connection—fostering feelings of warmth and safety, even when no one is physically present. For those who have endured neglect, trauma, or abandonment, this process can 'repattern' their relational experiences, allowing them to create new, healthier pathways of trust, care, and emotional safety.

The activation of mirror neurons also sheds light on why group therapy or partner-based visualization practices can amplify healing—by fostering a sense of shared connection and mutual support. When participants imagine themselves moving in sync with others or engaging in cooperative actions, the brain strengthens patterns of co-regulation and interpersonal connection, nurturing a deeper sense of belonging and empathy. This makes visualization not just an individual practice but a powerful relational tool, fostering a deeper sense of belonging and mutual empathy.

The power of visualization lies in its ability to engage both the brain and the body, creating real changes through imagined experience. Neuroplasticity allows the brain to rewire maladaptive patterns, the autonomic nervous system responds by restoring balance between fight-or-flight and rest-and-digest states, and mirror neurons enable clients to embody new ways of being, even without direct physical action.

Types of Visualization Techniques

Several visualization techniques can be utilized in somatic therapy, each serving a unique purpose. Here are a few common approaches:

Approach 1. Safe Place Visualization

Safe place visualization involves creating a mental image of a calming environment—somewhere you feel truly safe and at peace. It might be a serene beach, a quiet forest, or a cozy room filled with warmth and comfort. This technique can be particularly helpful during times of stress or anxiety. You might visualize a serene beach, a quiet forest, or a cozy room.

As you imagine this sanctuary, invite all your senses to come alive. What do you see? What sounds fill the air? What scents surround you? How does your body feel in this peaceful space?0020What do you see? Hear? Smell? Feel? Allow yourself to immerse fully in this visualization. The purpose is to create a mental sanctuary you can return to whenever you need a moment of peace.

Approach 2. Healing Light Visualization

Healing light visualization invites you to imagine a radiant, soothing light flowing through your body, easing any tension, pain, or discomfort. Visualize this light as a warm embrace, gently dissolving blocks and promoting healing. This technique often involves imagining a warm, bright light that envelops you, soothing any physical or emotional discomfort. You may visualize this light moving through areas of tension or pain, promoting relaxation and healing.

As you breathe deeply, imagine this light sinking into your very cells, carrying with it a sense of peace and relief. With each breath, feel the light dissolve any physical or emotional tension, leaving you lighter and more whole. You might notice a sense of release or relief as the healing light flows through you, facilitating emotional and physical well-being.

Approach 3. Emotion Exploration

Emotion exploration is about visualizing your feelings as colors, shapes, or textures. For instance, you might see sadness as a heavy blue cloud, or anxiety as a jagged red shape. This technique helps you step back and observe your emotions from a new perspective. This technique can help you gain a clearer understanding of your emotions. For example, you might picture sadness as a blue cloud or anxiety as a jagged red shape.

By representing your emotions through visuals, you gain distance from them, allowing you to explore their qualities without getting lost in the intensity. This process helps you understand your feelings more clearly and releases their grip on you. This process allows for greater clarity and helps you process your feelings more effectively.

Approach 4. Energy Flow Visualization

Energy flow visualization helps you picture the movement of energy through your body, like a gentle river winding its way through you or a soft breeze moving across your skin. This practice allows you to tune into your body's natural rhythms and restore harmony. You can picture energy as a flowing river, a gentle breeze, or any form that resonates with you.

By visualizing this flow, you can release tension and identify areas of stagnation. This allows you to restore balance, ease, and vitality throughout your body. It encourages you to become aware of any blockages or areas of stagnation, allowing you to release tension and restore the flow of energy.

CHAPTER 6
THE ROLE OF CREATIVITY AND PLAY

Like many adults, I often overlooked the importance of simply taking time to have fun, to mess around and play. Life gets busy, and play can feel like a luxury, something that's only for children. But I was about to learn, through my work with clients, that play is not just for kids—it's essential for healing at any age. Even when I studied about the importance of play, I personally wasn't convinced. But as I used those principles with my clients, I was soon convinced of its impact.

When Mia, a 10-year-old girl, first came to see me, she sat quietly on the edge of the couch, her shoulders slumped, her gaze fixed on the floor. Her mother explained that Mia hadn't been the same since their family moved to New York a few months earlier. Once a bubbly and curious child, Mia had withdrawn socially, lost interest in activities she once loved, and stopped engaging with her peers.

"She used to be so full of life," her mother said, her voice full of sadness. "Now, she barely speaks or plays. I feel like we've lost a part of her."

Mia wasn't showing typical signs of anxiety or depression, but there was a deep sense of something missing. Her spark, her curiosity, and her love for play had dimmed, leaving her quiet and withdrawn. Her parents hoped that therapy could help her reconnect with herself and others. I knew that for Mia, the way forward wasn't through lengthy conversations or forced structure. For a child like her, the language of healing would come through creativity, play, and the freedom to express what couldn't be put into words. Play is the natural language of children, and in somatic therapy, it becomes a way for the body to express, release, and heal what words cannot.

In our first session, my goal was simple: to create a safe, inviting space where Mia could explore—without pressure or expectations—both physically and emotionally. I wanted her to feel free to engage with whatever sparked her curiosity, without judgment. I didn't want to rush her into sharing or moving; instead, I followed her lead. The room was filled with sensory objects—feathers, sand trays, colorful scarves, clay, and soft balls.

When Mia entered the space, I encouraged her to explore anything that caught her eye. At first, she was hesitant. She picked up a soft ball and squeezed it a few times but quickly put it down. I noticed her body language—her posture remained stiff, her movements cautious. It was as if she didn't trust herself to engage with the world around her.

I gently invited her to sit on the floor with me. I started rolling a small ball back and forth, modeling a slow, rhythmic movement. I didn't need her to do exactly as I did, just be curious enough to engage however she wanted to.

After a few moments of watching me, Mia tentatively reached for the ball and rolled it back. We spent a while in silence, just rolling the ball between us. This simple act of movement—just rolling the ball back and forth—became a bridge for Mia to reconnect, not only with me but with her own body. Slowly, she began to feel her body again, to trust it, and to recognize it as a source of expression and joy.

As we continued, I added playful elements. I pretended the ball was a mischievous animal, giving it a personality, which made Mia smile for the first time since she walked into my office. Her shoulders relaxed, and she started to giggle softly. Gradually, I saw her movements become more expressive—she began tossing the ball, catching it, and adding her own creative twists.

This playful interaction wasn't just fun—it was somatic healing in action. Through play, Mia's body began releasing the tension it had been holding since the move. Play allowed Mia to access the emotions that had been buried under layers of fear, confusion, and stress. It wasn't through words—it was through spontaneous, joyful movement that she began to release and express what had been trapped inside her body. The rhythmic tossing, catching, and rolling of the ball helped regulate Mia's nervous system. The repetition of the motion, the feel of the ball in her hands, and the slow, steady pace soothed her body and mind, bringing her back to a place of balance and calm.

In a later session, I introduced a new element—art and creative storytelling. I asked Mia if she wanted to draw a picture of how she was feeling. She chose a box of crayons and began to draw slowly, first sketching a dark cloud. As Mia worked, I stayed with her, gently reflecting on what I noticed in her drawing. I could see the weight of the cloud, the dark strokes she used, and I wanted her to feel seen without having to explain anything. "That cloud looks heavy," I said. "What else could we add to the picture to help the cloud feel better?"

Mia paused, as if contemplating the possibilities. Then, with a deep breath, she picked up a bright yellow crayon, as if she were choosing light to balance out the heaviness. "Maybe it needs the sun," she said quietly, adding rays around a smiling sun. Through this creative process, Mia was expressing emotions she couldn't put into words—she was letting her feelings flow onto the page, safely and on her own terms. It was a powerful release, a way to let the emotions move through her without the weight of judgment.

We took the exercise a step further, turning the sun and the cloud into characters with personalities. This wasn't just a drawing anymore—it became a conversation, a playful narrative that allowed Mia to explore complex emotions with curiosity, humor, and creativity. I asked, "What does the cloud need to feel lighter?" Mia laughed and said, "The sun needs to tickle it!" This playful storytelling allowed her to explore complex emotions—like sadness and hope—without pressure or judgment. It also gave her a sense of agency—the ability to imagine, change, and shift her emotional landscape.

As Mia grew more comfortable in our sessions, something beautiful began to happen: her movements became more fluid, more spontaneous. She danced with the scarves, pretending to fly like a bird, each movement an expression of newfound freedom. These playful acts were her body's way of reawakening to joy, to trust, and to self-expression. She danced with the colorful scarves, pretended to fly like a bird, and built small sandcastles in the sand tray. With every playful movement, she was engaging in nervous system regulation—moving between states of activation (excitement) and relaxation (calm).

To help her integrate what she experienced in therapy, I encouraged Mia's family to embrace unstructured play at home, setting aside time for spontaneous dance parties, storytelling games, and simple co-regulation activities. These practices were more than just fun—they were ways to rebuild connection, trust, and a sense of safety in the family unit. I encouraged them to set aside time for unstructured play, like spontaneous dance parties or storytelling games. I also suggested simple co-regulation activities, like playing catch or synchronized movement (clapping rhythms or walking side by side), to rebuild connection and trust within the family.

I explained to her mother that play is not just a child's pastime—it is a powerful tool for self-expression, healing, and connection. Through play, Mia was learning to trust her body again, reconnect with joy, and engage with the world in a way that felt safe and exciting.

Reflections and the Path Forward

After a few months, Mia began to show noticeable changes. She started talking more at school, re-engaged with her art projects, and asked her mother if they could explore the parks in their new neighborhood. In our sessions, she moved freely—jumping, spinning, and laughing. She was no longer the withdrawn child who had first come to me; she was playful, curious, and connected with herself again.

Mia's story teaches me that healing doesn't always come from pushing through serious work—it thrives in moments of joy, spontaneity, and creativity. The playful moments, the lightness of movement, and the laughter all serve as profound healing forces that allow the nervous system to reset and rebuild. The principles of somatic therapy teach us that movement and play are essential parts of regulating the nervous system, especially for children. Play creates a space where emotions can flow, tension can release, and connection can rebuild.

Mia's journey highlights several key somatic therapy principles, each one playing a crucial role in her recovery:

- Attunement and Following the Body's Lead: By letting Mia take the lead and engage at her own pace, we created a space of safety, building trust in both herself and the therapeutic process.

- Co-Regulation Through Play: Our playful interactions didn't just support Mia—they regulated both of us. Our shared laughter and play built a connection that transcended words.

- Creativity as Emotional Expression: Drawing, storytelling, and play became Mia's language for expressing emotions that words couldn't fully capture. These creative outlets allowed her to process and release feelings she couldn't articulate.

- Rhythmic Movement for Regulation: Simple, repetitive movements like tossing the ball and dancing with scarves helped Mia's nervous system reset, bringing balance and emotional regulation.

- Integration into Daily Life: The power of play and creativity didn't stay confined to our sessions. Mia took these practices home, using them to stay grounded and connected to her emotions and family.Mia's case shows how play and creativity are essential tools in somatic therapy, especially for children. Movement, imagination, and spontaneous joy allow the nervous system to reset, creating a sense of safety and connection. Through creativity and playful exploration, Mia rediscovered her joy and self-connection. Her journey teaches me, time and again, that healing doesn't always require effort or struggle; it happens when we allow ourselves to play, to be curious, to move, and to express freely without judgment.

Whether it's through a game, a dance, or a simple drawing, the body speaks through play—and when we listen, profound healing becomes possible.

The Importance of Play in Healing

Play is more than just an activity—it's a vital part of the healing journey. It's a space where we can reconnect with our true selves, where vulnerability and joy can coexist, and where the body and mind find room to breathe and heal. In the safe space created by play, emotions can surface without fear of judgment. This space invites self-expression and provides the opportunity to confront painful feelings in a way that feels manageable, easing the emotional burden that trauma often leaves behind. When engaged in playful activities, you create a space where vulnerability is welcomed. This environment encourages you to express emotions freely, facilitating authentic self-exploration. In such a setting, you can confront difficult feelings, process experiences, and cultivate resilience.

For those recovering from trauma, play becomes more than just an activity—it's a gateway to releasing held tension and processing buried emotions. In these playful moments, the body and mind learn to trust the process of healing, bit by bit, through gentle exploration. During play, the brain enters a relaxed state, reducing anxiety and promoting a sense of calm. This state is conducive to emotional exploration, enabling you to access deeper layers of your psyche. You may find that engaging in play helps to dismantle emotional barriers, fostering connection to your inner self and others.

Research backs the idea that play isn't just for enjoyment—it's a powerful catalyst for growth and healing. Through playful experiences, the brain's capacity for neuroplasticity allows us to rewire entrenched emotional responses, creating new neural pathways that reinforce positive coping mechanisms and healthier emotional patterns. Studies have shown that engaging in playful activities stimulates the brain's reward system, leading to the release of endorphins. These natural chemicals enhance mood and reduce feelings of stress and anxiety. Moreover, play is closely linked to neuroplasticity, which is the brain's ability to reorganize itself by forming new neural connections throughout life.

Neuroplasticity is crucial for healing from trauma. When you engage in playful experiences, your brain becomes more flexible and adaptive. This flexibility allows you to rewire negative thought patterns and emotional responses, fostering resilience. Children who engage in imaginative play demonstrate improved problem-solving skills and emotional regulation. This research suggests that play not only enhances cognitive development but also contributes to emotional well-being.

In conclusion, play and creativity are not merely distractions—they are essential tools for emotional healing and personal growth. They invite us into a state of openness, where the mind, body, and heart can reconnect, explore, and ultimately, heal. By embracing the playful and creative parts of ourselves, we rediscover the joy of being fully present and resilient in the face of life's challenges. It creates a safe and open environment for emotional exploration, promotes neuroplasticity, and enhances resilience. By incorporating exploration into therapeutic practices, individuals can access deeper layers of their emotional landscape, facilitating healing and personal growth.

Creative Expression as a Somatic Tool

Engaging in creative activities—whether through art, dance, or music—offers a profound way to process trauma. These outlets provide a safe space for expressing emotions that may otherwise remain locked inside, unspoken and untapped. Creativity gives voice to the unspeakable, allowing your body and mind to heal through nonverbal expression. These creative outlets provide unique pathways for self-exploration and healing, allowing you to connect with your inner self in ways that words often cannot convey. By tapping into your creativity, you can access deep emotions and release feelings trapped in the body, facilitating emotional regulation and growth.

Art therapy is one powerful avenue for creative expression. Artistic activities, such as painting, drawing, or sculpting, tap into your subconscious, allowing emotions to emerge through the medium of color, shape, and texture. What you create on the canvas can become an external reflection of your inner world, offering clarity and release. Through this process, you not only express but also process deep, often hidden, emotions. This nonverbal form of expression can reveal hidden feelings and insights about your experiences.

A good way to do this would be to ask yourself, 'What would your anxiety look like as a drawing?' You might choose dark colors and chaotic shapes, reflecting your emotional state. As you create, you gain awareness of these feelings, which can lead to deeper understanding and processing.

A creative exercise that encourages body awareness in art therapy is "body mapping." In this activity, you create a large outline of your body on paper and fill in the sections with colors, images, or words that represent how you feel physically and emotionally. This process allows you to visualize your experiences and connect with areas of tension or discomfort in your body. As you fill in your body map, you may uncover emotions tied to specific physical sensations or areas of discomfort in your body. This can offer deep insights into how unresolved emotions manifest physically. By acknowledging these areas and connecting them to your emotional experiences, you begin to integrate the healing process, allowing your body to release what it has been holding.

Dance is another powerful medium for emotional expression. Dance is not only a physical expression—it is an emotional release. Through movement, you can free yourself from the pent-up emotions that your body has been storing, reconnecting with the fluidity and joy of being alive. Somatic dance practices, like Authentic Movement or 5Rhythms, help you explore the full spectrum of your emotions by inviting your body to move without restrictions, expressing what words cannot. Somatic dance practices, such as Authentic Movement or 5Rhythms, encourage free expression and exploration of physical sensations. These practices invite you to move intuitively, following the impulses of your body without judgment or expectation.

Music is a universal language, one that speaks directly to the heart. Whether listening, singing, or playing, music can evoke emotions in a way that words alone often cannot. The rhythm, melody, and lyrics can mirror your emotional state, allowing you to process feelings like grief, joy, or anger. Music becomes both a tool for release and an avenue for self-reflection, helping you connect with your emotions and find healing through sound. Whether listening to music, singing, or playing an instrument, music has the power to evoke deep emotional responses. You can experiment with sounds (like humming, clapping, or drumming) to express emotions and shift energy. It can serve as a cathartic outlet, helping you process feelings of joy, grief, or anger. For example, you might create a playlist of songs that resonate with your emotional state and use it as a backdrop for a reflective journaling session. This combination can deepen your understanding of your emotions and enhance your self-awareness.

Another creative exercise involving music is songwriting. Writing lyrics can be a powerful way to articulate feelings that are difficult to express verbally. You might start by jotting down words or phrases that capture your emotional landscape and then craft them into a song. The process of songwriting or engaging with music in any form can bring profound clarity to your emotions. It not only helps you articulate feelings that are hard to express, but it also offers a powerful release—freeing the emotions that have been confined within. Through this creative outlet, you not only understand your emotional landscape better but begin to heal, one note at a time.

CHAPTER 7
PROGRESSIVE MUSCLE RELAXATION

When Marcus, a 29-year-old professional tennis player, walked into my office, I could immediately sense his exhaustion. His body seemed drained—not just physically, but emotionally. His shoulders were drawn up toward his ears, his jaw clenched, and there was a palpable tension in his posture, even as he sat. It was as if his body was constantly preparing for something, never quite at ease. His shoulders were rigid, his jaw tight, and even in rest, his muscles seemed braced for action. He explained that despite being at the peak of his career, his body had started to betray him. Chronic muscle tightness and fatigue were affecting his performance, and no amount of stretching, physical therapy, or massage provided lasting relief.

"I've tried everything—sports therapy, acupuncture, even counseling," he said with frustration. "Nothing sticks. My body just won't relax."

1. Understanding the Root of Muscle Tension

As Marcus shared his story, I recognized a familiar pattern: his body was trapped in a chronic fight-or-flight state. This constant activation of the sympathetic nervous system meant that his muscles were always on alert—contracting, tightening, preparing for the next match, competition, or stressor. His nervous system had learned to remain in this state, even during moments of rest. Years of high-pressure tournaments had conditioned his nervous system to stay in an activated state. Even during downtime, his body couldn't switch off, as if it didn't know how to relax without a structured goal.

I explained that somatic therapy focuses on integrating the body and nervous system, guiding them back to a state of balance. One of the techniques I wanted to introduce was Progressive Muscle Relaxation (PMR), a method designed to help the body experience the contrast between tension and relaxation. Through this practice, we can begin to reset the nervous system's response to stress. This method involves intentionally tensing and then releasing different muscle groups, helping the body learn to distinguish between tension and relaxation. "The goal," I said, "is to help your body re-learn how to relax—not just during therapy, but whenever you need it."

Marcus was skeptical at first, raising an eyebrow. 'You think squeezing my muscles will help me relax?' he asked, as if trying to figure out how something so simple could work. His body language suggested doubt—his arms still crossed in defense, his posture tense, as though he couldn't quite believe that relaxation could come from such a straightforward practice. I smiled and said, “It’s not just about squeezing—it’s about teaching your body to let go.”

2. The Progressive Muscle Relaxation Process

We began the PMR practice lying down on a mat, with Marcus in a comfortable position. I invited him to close his eyes and take a few slow, deep breaths to settle into the space. Then, we moved systematically through different muscle groups, starting with his feet and gradually working up to his shoulders, neck, and face.

“On your next inhale, squeeze your feet tightly—imagine you’re gripping the ground beneath you,” I instructed. “Hold the tension for a few seconds... now exhale slowly and release, letting the muscles melt.” We repeated this process, muscle group by muscle group, with Marcus tensing and releasing his calves, thighs, abdomen, and arms.

At first, Marcus struggled with the exercise, overcompensating by holding the tension too tightly in his muscles and then releasing abruptly. I could see the discomfort on his face—his brow furrowed in concentration, his body tensing even more than needed, as if he was trying to control the release rather than letting it happen naturally. “I don’t think I’m doing this right,” he said. I reminded him that PMR isn’t about perfection—it’s about learning to feel the difference between tension and relaxation. Over time, his body began to respond. His movements became smoother, and he started to release each muscle group more intentionally.

After 30 minutes, we ended the session with a full-body scan, inviting Marcus to notice any shifts in sensation. He took a deep breath, then exhaled slowly. ‘My shoulders feel lower,’ he said, a note of surprise in his voice. ‘Like I finally dropped them, but I didn’t even realize I was holding them up.’ It was as though his body had been carrying an invisible weight, one that he could now begin to put down.

3. Releasing Emotional Tension Stored in the Body

In the next few sessions, as Marcus became more comfortable with PMR, we started to explore the emotional underpinnings of his chronic tension. The body holds onto stress, fear, and expectations—especially in high-pressure environments like professional sports. Through the progressive relaxation practice, Marcus began to notice emotions surfacing as he released different parts of his body.

During one session, as we focused on his hands—muscles crucial to his sport—Marcus let out a long, shaky breath. His fingers twitched slightly, as if reluctant to let go. ‘I feel...sad,’ he admitted, his voice quieter than usual. ‘I never realized how tired I am from holding on all the time.’ He flexed his fingers again, slower this time, as if sensing their weight for the first time. His shoulders slumped, and for a brief moment, he simply sat with the feeling.

By creating space for these emotions through the PMR practice, Marcus realized that his body wasn't just tight—it was carrying years of expectation, pressure, and unspoken fatigue. Each time he tensed and released a muscle, it wasn't just physical—it was his body's way of telling a story he had never listened to before. Relaxation, he learned, wasn't just about stretching—it was about giving himself permission to feel, to release, to be.

4. Integrating Relaxation into His Daily Routine

One of the challenges Marcus faced was that his nervous system was always "on," even during non-competitive periods. To help him integrate relaxation into his routine, I suggested that he practice PMR for just 10 minutes every evening, using it as a way to signal to his body that the day was winding down. I also encouraged him to incorporate micro-relaxation techniques during key moments in his routine—clenching and releasing his hands before a serve, rolling his shoulders between sets, or taking slow, deep breaths in the locker room. These weren't just relaxation techniques; they were cues to remind his body that it was safe to soften, even in the midst of high-stakes competition.

As we progressed, Marcus became more attuned to his body. He could catch tension building up throughout the day and release it before it became overwhelming. "I used to think that relaxing meant doing nothing," he reflected during one session. "But now I see it's something I have to practice, just like my game."

5. Results: Restoring Flow and Freedom

After a few months of working together, Marcus noticed profound shifts in both his body and mind. The chronic tightness in his shoulders and neck eased, and he found himself performing better on the court—not because he was pushing harder, but because his body felt lighter and more responsive.

During one follow-up session, Marcus leaned forward, his eyes bright with excitement. "It was the third set, and I was about to serve," he recalled. "I felt it—the tightness creeping into my fingers, that familiar tension locking my wrist. Normally, I would've powered through, forcing my way past it. But this time, I paused. I took a slow breath, tensed my hand just enough to feel it, then released. And just like that—something shifted. My grip softened, my shoulders loosened, and when I tossed the ball into the air, it felt effortless. I wasn't fighting my body anymore—I was working with it."

PMR not only improved Marcus's performance but also gave him a new sense of trust in his body. He no longer felt trapped by tension, knowing that he could release it whenever he needed.

6. Reflections and Takeaways

Marcus's journey reminded me that the body needs permission to relax. We live in a world that celebrates pushing through discomfort—whether in sports, careers, or everyday responsibilities. But without rest, the body begins to push back. PMR didn't just help Marcus physically—it rewrote the way he related to his own body. Instead of treating tension as an obstacle, he began to see relaxation as a skill, one just as valuable as his training regimen. His story is proof that learning to let go is just as powerful as learning to hold on.

His story also reinforced a valuable lesson: Relaxation is not the absence of effort; it's the presence of awareness. Through somatic practices like PMR, we can help the body remember how to soften, let go, and move freely again. Marcus didn't just regain his physical strength—he rediscovered ease, trust, and balance in his body, setting the foundation for a healthier career and life ahead.

What is Progressive Muscle Relaxation (PMR)?

Have you ever noticed how your shoulders stay tense, even when you're not stressed? Or how your jaw remains clenched long after a difficult conversation? This kind of tension often lingers without us realizing it. Progressive Muscle Relaxation (PMR) is a simple yet powerful technique designed to break this cycle, helping you release built-up tension and reconnect with your body.

In the 1920s, Dr. Edmund Jacobson, a physician and researcher, noticed something intriguing: his patients who reported chronic stress also had persistently tight muscles. He found that by teaching them to tense and then release different muscle groups, their anxiety levels dropped. His discovery led to Progressive Muscle Relaxation (PMR), a method that has since become a cornerstone of stress management and therapeutic healing.

For many trauma survivors, physical tension becomes a constant companion. Imagine someone who grew up in an unpredictable household—always bracing for the next outburst. Over time, their shoulders stay tight, their stomach clenches, and their breathing becomes shallow, even when no threat is present. PMR offers a way back into the body, gently guiding individuals to notice these areas of tension and, most importantly, teaching them how to release it.

PMR also works by resetting the delicate balance between the sympathetic nervous system (SNS)—which triggers fight-or-flight—and the parasympathetic nervous system (PNS)—which promotes rest-and-digest functions. Think of your nervous system like a car with two gears: the gas pedal (SNS) and the brakes (PNS). Many people dealing with chronic stress or trauma have their foot stuck on the gas, constantly revving their engine. PMR works by briefly pressing the gas (tensing muscles) and then consciously applying the brakes (releasing tension), teaching the body how to shift gears naturally.

By repeatedly practicing PMR, you train your body to recognize the difference between tension and relaxation, making it easier to release stress even in difficult moments. Over time, this simple practice builds a sense of control over both body and mind.

Whether you're navigating daily stress, recovering from trauma, or simply seeking a deeper connection with yourself, PMR is a tool that can help you reclaim ease, balance, and presence in your life.

Adapting PMR for Specific Populations and Needs

Progressive Muscle Relaxation (PMR) is a powerful tool for releasing tension, but not all bodies experience tension the same way. A trauma survivor may need a gentler approach, an athlete might use it to enhance performance, and someone with chronic pain may need modifications to avoid discomfort. By adapting PMR to individual needs, we can make relaxation more accessible, effective, and empowering for everyone.

For trauma survivors, tensing and releasing muscles can sometimes evoke sensations that feel overwhelming or unsafe. Trauma often leaves the body in a state of hypervigilance, making physical engagement feel threatening rather than relaxing.

For example, a survivor of a car accident may feel uneasy tensing their legs, as it reminds them of the physical bracing during impact. In this case, we might start with small, non-triggering muscle groups—like the hands or shoulders—or use visualization instead of physical engagement. Another approach is focusing on slow, intentional breathing alongside PMR to create a sense of control. By modifying the practice, trauma survivors can reconnect with their bodies at a safe, manageable pace.

For individuals with anxiety, PMR offers an immediate way to break the cycle of tension before it spirals into panic. By recognizing early signs—like a clenched jaw or tight shoulders—clients can apply PMR in real-time to regain a sense of control.

Anxiety often keeps the nervous system stuck in a heightened state of arousal, making it difficult to relax. PMR counteracts this by systematically engaging and relaxing the muscles, activating the parasympathetic nervous system (which promotes rest and digestion). Over time, this practice rewires the nervous system, making relaxation a more natural response. Many clients find PMR particularly useful before sleep, as it helps them shift out of nighttime anxiety and into deeper rest.

Pain often causes the body to unconsciously tighten muscles in an attempt to protect the affected area, which paradoxically increases discomfort. PMR helps by interrupting this pain-tension cycle, but modifications are necessary for those with chronic pain.

Instead of tensing the painful area, we might focus on surrounding muscle groups—like relaxing the hips to ease lower back pain. In some cases, clients may only visualize the process at first, training their bodies to expect relief before engaging physically. By gradually introducing gentle engagement, individuals with chronic pain can regain a sense of ease and control over their bodies.

High-level athletes often carry tension throughout their bodies due to intense training schedules, competitive stress, and physical exertion. While this tension is necessary during performance, it becomes counterproductive when it lingers.

Before a big game, an athlete might unknowingly hold tension in their hands or shoulders, reducing agility. PMR helps them scan for unnecessary tension and release it, improving reaction time and efficiency. After competition, PMR aids muscle recovery by improving circulation and reducing soreness, allowing the body to heal more effectively. When integrated into daily routines, PMR helps athletes achieve a sustainable balance between training, recovery, and relaxation, reducing the risk of injury and burnout. By tailoring PMR to meet the unique needs of trauma survivors, individuals with anxiety, chronic pain sufferers, and athletes, we ensure that the practice remains effective and accessible. These thoughtful modifications transform PMR into a versatile tool for self-regulation, healing, and performance. No matter where you start, PMR offers a pathway to reconnect with your body, release tension, and cultivate a deeper sense of ease

CHAPTER 8
INTEGRATING OTHER MODALITIES TO ENHANCE SOMATIC THERAPY

Healing is never a straight path—it's a weaving journey that often requires different tools at different times. Over the years, I've found that blending somatic therapy with other modalities allows clients to access healing in ways that feel natural to them. Whether through mindfulness, movement, or creative expression, integrating these approaches enriches the somatic experience, offering new ways to process emotions, self-regulate, and reconnect with the body.

Example 1: Mindfulness and Somatic Therapy for Chronic Pain

One of my clients, Rachel, Rachel had lived with chronic neck and shoulder pain for years. Every stressful moment—from work deadlines to personal worries—seemed to tighten the grip her body held on her pain. She had tried physical therapy and even medication, but nothing provided lasting relief.

In our sessions, we discovered that her pain wasn't just physical—it was deeply tied to unprocessed emotions. While somatic therapy helped her recognize her body's stress response, integrating mindfulness meditation allowed her to observe her sensations without judgment. By practicing non-reactivity toward her pain, she stopped bracing against it and instead allowed it to shift.

"For the first time," she told me, "I don't feel like I'm fighting my own body."

Over time, her pain episodes became less frequent and intense, allowing her to move through life with greater ease.

Example 2: Expressive Arts with Somatic Therapy for Emotional Trauma

Leo, a 32-year-old artist, came to me with a grief that felt too heavy to put into words. After losing his father, he found himself creatively blocked—unable to paint, write, or express the emotions that churned inside him. While somatic therapy helped him identify where grief lived in his body, it was through expressive arts therapy that he finally found release.

We combined movement with drawing, allowing him to translate his emotions into color and form. One day, as he finished a painting, he exhaled deeply and said, "This feels like I finally said what I couldn't before."

By the end of our work together, Leo had not only processed his grief but had also reclaimed his artistic voice. His art became a bridge between past pain and present healing, allowing him to express what words alone could not.

Combining Somatic Therapy with Talk Therapy and Other Modalities

Integrating somatic therapy with talk therapy offers a more comprehensive approach to healing. Talk therapy allows you to explore emotions verbally, while somatic therapy connects you to the physical sensations accompanying those emotions. This dual focus strengthens emotional awareness, helping you recognize how your body responds to thoughts and feelings. For instance, as you discuss a stressful experience, you might notice tightness in your chest or tension in your jaw. Becoming aware of these sensations leads to deeper healing by promoting insight into how emotions manifest physically and enabling their release.

Practical strategies for integrating somatic techniques into talk therapy include paying attention to bodily responses during sessions. If you feel disconnected or struggle to articulate emotions, pausing to focus on your body can be helpful. For example, while discussing anxiety, you might take a moment to notice where tension resides in your body. Communication about these sensations also enriches therapy. Expressing, "I feel heaviness in my chest," creates a bridge between physical experience and emotional awareness, enhancing the therapeutic dialogue. Incorporating breathwork into sessions—such as deep, intentional breathing—grounds you, calms the nervous system, and fosters deeper processing. Additionally, movement practices, such as stretching or gentle gestures between conversations, can release stored tension and facilitate emotional expression.

EMDR and Somatic Therapy: Processing Trauma with the Body

EMDR (Eye Movement Desensitization and Reprocessing) is an evidence-based therapy for trauma, using bilateral stimulation (such as guided eye movements) to help reprocess distressing memories. Somatic therapy enhances EMDR by ensuring the body remains grounded and present.

- **Before EMDR:** Grounding techniques (deep breathing, visualization, body scanning) help regulate the nervous system.
- **During EMDR:** Clients track physical sensations linked to traumatic memories, allowing for more complete processing.
- **After EMDR:** Movement practices like stretching or rhythmic rocking help the nervous system return to balance.

By integrating these two approaches, trauma processing becomes more holistic and embodied, reducing emotional overwhelm.

CBT and Somatic Therapy: Changing Thought Patterns and Body Responses

Cognitive Behavioral Therapy (CBT), when combined with somatic therapy, enhances emotional regulation by addressing both thoughts and body sensations. While CBT focuses on shifting negative thinking patterns, integrating somatic practices ensures that the physical responses accompanying these thoughts are acknowledged and released. For example, as you challenge a negative thought, you might notice tension in your shoulders or tightness in your chest. Becoming aware of these physical sensations allows you to release them through breathwork or gentle stretches, promoting a sense of calm. This dual focus fosters deeper healing by addressing the emotional and physical dimensions of stress.

Combining somatic therapy with these modalities offers a holistic approach to well-being. Whether through talk therapy, EMDR, or CBT, incorporating body awareness techniques strengthens your ability to regulate emotions and process difficult experiences. This integrative approach helps you reconnect with your body, fostering emotional resilience and promoting lasting change.

Challenges and Solutions in Combining Modalities

As you explore somatic therapy combined with other approaches, it's normal to feel a bit overwhelmed at first. Sometimes, too many techniques are introduced too quickly, making it hard to stay connected to what feels helpful. A good therapist will work with you at your pace, checking in regularly to ensure the process feels manageable and aligned with your needs.

It's also important to know that not every modality will resonate with you—and that's perfectly okay. Some people feel drawn to mindfulness or yoga, while others find expressive arts or breathwork more effective. Therapy is a collaborative journey, and experimenting without pressure is key. If a particular technique doesn't feel right, share your thoughts. Your therapist will help you explore alternatives, so you can discover what works best. Ultimately, the goal is to find a rhythm that feels supportive, helping you heal and reconnect with your body in ways that feel natural and meaningful.

BOOK 2

Exercises

CHAPTER 1
EXPLORING THE CONNECTION OF MIND AND BODY

Imagine lying down after a long, stressful day. Your shoulders ache, your jaw feels tight, and your mind is running in circles. But as you slowly shift your focus inward—scanning your body from head to toe—you begin to notice something remarkable: your body is carrying tension you didn't even realize was there. With every breath, you release a little more, letting go of stress one muscle at a time. This is the power of the Mind-Body Scan.

In this chapter, we explore a powerful combination of **body scanning** and **stretching exercises** designed to promote deep awareness and relaxation. The integration of these two techniques allows you to connect with your body on a deeper level, uncover areas of tension, and release physical and emotional stress stored within.

Body scanning helps you notice **subtle sensations**, revealing where tension is held. Stretching, on the other hand, provides **an active way** to release this tension, encouraging flexibility and mobility. Together, these practices create a harmonious balance between mind and body.

Exercise: Mind-Body Scan

1. Overview of the Mind-Body Scan

The Mind-Body Scan is a powerful practice that nurtures awareness of both physical sensations and emotions. It helps release built-up tension, leading to relaxation and mental clarity. This exercise invites you to connect with your body in a non-judgmental way, fostering a sense of mindfulness and inner calm.

2. Starting the Practice: Setting the Stage

Find a quiet space where you can sit or lie down comfortably. Once settled, close your eyes if it feels natural. Begin by taking deep breaths: inhale through your nose, letting your abdomen expand, and exhale slowly through your mouth, releasing any tension. Allow yourself to feel supported by the surface beneath you, grounding yourself in the moment.

3. Conducting the Body Scan

Begin at the top of your head, gently noticing any areas of tension. Progress downward—soften your forehead, unclench your jaw, and let your shoulders relax. Visualize tension leaving your body as you breathe out. Move your attention through each body part: arms, chest, abdomen, legs, and finally, your feet. With each exhale, imagine warmth spreading through your muscles, leaving them heavy and relaxed.

4. Completing the Experience and Returning

After scanning your entire body, spend a few moments appreciating the calm you've cultivated. Compare how your body feels now with how it felt at the start. When ready, slowly return your awareness to the present—wiggle your fingers and toes, take a deep breath, and open your eyes. Incorporate the Mind-Body Scan into your routine to manage stress, building deeper awareness with regular practice. sensations and promotes relaxation, enabling you to navigate challenging emotions with greater ease.

Exercise: Tension and Release Through Stretching

1. Overview of Stretching for Emotional Release

Stretching for Emotional Release blends mindful movement with breath, providing an opportunity to release both physical and emotional tension. This somatic therapy encourages awareness of how emotions are stored within the body, helping you foster relaxation, balance, and emotional freedom. Through intentional stretches, it invites you to connect with your body and breath in a healing and empowering way.

2. Creating a Comfortable Space for Stretching

Begin by finding a quiet space where you can move freely. Depending on the stretches, you may choose to stand, sit, or lie down. Wear comfortable clothing that won't restrict your movements. Take a few deep breaths: inhale deeply through your nose, expanding your chest, and exhale slowly through your mouth, releasing tension and setting the tone for your practice.

3. Neck and Shoulder Stretches to Relieve Stored Stress

Start by tilting your head gently to one side, bringing your ear toward your shoulder, and holding the stretch for several breaths. With each exhale, visualize tension draining from your neck. Repeat on the other side. For your shoulders, raise one arm overhead and bend your elbow, placing your hand behind your neck. Use your other hand to gently pull on your elbow, feeling the stretch deepen. Repeat on the opposite side, exhaling tension away with each breath.

4. Deepening Relaxation with Full-Body Stretches

Transition into a side stretch by raising your right arm and bending to the left, opening space along your torso. Switch sides to maintain balance, focusing on releasing tension along the sides of your body. For hip and thigh stretches, step one foot forward while bending your front knee slightly. Sink into the stretch, letting tightness ease with every exhale. Shift your focus to the hamstrings and calves by extending one leg forward and folding at the hips. Reach toward your toes, breathing deeply to allow your muscles to relax further.

5. Completing the Practice and Building Consistency

End your session with a full-body stretch: stand tall, raise both arms overhead, and feel the lengthening from your toes to your fingertips. Inhale deeply and, with each exhale, release any lingering tension. Slowly lower your arms and return to a neutral stance. Take a moment to notice how your body feels now compared to when you started. Incorporating these stretches into your routine will improve body awareness, helping you release built-up emotions and better manage stress over time.

Exercise: Body Mapping

Body Mapping for Emotional Identification is a somatic therapy exercise designed to help you connect with and understand your emotions as they manifest in your body. This practice encourages self-awareness, allowing you to identify where emotions are stored physically and to gain insight into how they influence your overall well-being.

1. Prepare Your Materials

Gather a body template from resources online or use the one below. Have colored pencils, markers, or other tools ready to draw shapes, textures, or marks on the template.

2. Set an Intention for the Exercise

Decide what aspect of your emotional or physical experience you want to explore (e.g., tension, stress, or recent changes). This intention will guide your focus as you fill out the body map.

3. Map Your Body's Sensations

Use colors, patterns, and symbols to represent sensations, emotions, or areas of tension in your body. Focus on how these experiences feel rather than trying to label them with words.

4. Reflect on Your Experience

Once the body map is complete, review the areas you've marked. Notice any patterns, shapes, or colors that stand out. Pay attention to how the process made you feel.

5. Describe Your Body Map in Your Own Words

Without pressure to use specific language, describe what each part of your map represents. Feel free to use colors, symbols, or metaphors that resonate with you.

6. Share and Explore

If working with a coach or therapist, explain your body map. They will guide you through reflection and inquiry, helping you connect with underlying emotions or sensations without offering their own interpretations.

7. Use the Map as a Communication Tool

Continue using your map's symbols or language throughout your self-exploration or therapy. These visual representations can serve as a helpful way to communicate emotions that might otherwise be difficult to express.

CHAPTER 2
VISUALIZATION FOR MANAGING INTRUSIVE THOUGHTS

Imagine standing on a quiet beach. The waves roll in, slow and steady, as you feel the soft sand beneath your feet. The sound of the ocean fills your ears, and with each breath, your mind feels lighter. The tension fades. Your thoughts settle, like pebbles sinking into the water.

This is the power of visualization. It allows you to step away from overwhelming thoughts and enter a space of calm. Instead of battling intrusive thoughts, you can redirect your mind to something soothing and safe.

Visualization is a powerful tool for managing intrusive thoughts. It uses your imagination to create safe and calming experiences, engaging your brain in a way that reduces stress and anxiety. When you visualize peaceful scenarios, your nervous system responds as if you are truly there, helping you shift your focus and regain control.

Guided imagery helps you engage your senses, anchoring you in the present moment rather than letting intrusive thoughts take over. Over time, you can build mental "safe spaces"—places you can retreat to whenever you feel overwhelmed. These visualizations act as a tool to manage stress, regulate emotions, and bring your nervous system back into balance.

How Visualization Works in the Brain

Your brain doesn't fully distinguish between imagined and real experiences. When you visualize a calming scene, the same neural pathways activate as if you were truly there. This means that by engaging in visualization, you can shift your nervous system out of stress mode and into relaxation mode.

By practicing this regularly, you train your brain to respond differently to stress and intrusive thoughts, reducing their emotional grip over time.

Benefits of Visualization for Intrusive Thoughts

Visualization isn't just about escape; it's about rewiring your response to stress. Here's how guided imagery helps:

- **Reduces anxiety** – Shifting focus signals safety to your nervous system.
- **Enhances emotional regulation** – Helps replace distress with calm.
- **Improves focus and clarity** – Redirects attention, preventing obsessive thought loops.
- **Builds resilience** – Creates a mental 'safe space' you can return to anytime.

The more you use visualization, the more effective it becomes in managing difficult emotions and thoughts.

Exercise: Safe Space Visualization

This exercise helps you create a mental sanctuary—a place of absolute safety and calm. This is your personal retreat, a space where you can let go of stress and intrusive thoughts.

1. Find a Quiet, Comfortable Space

- Sit or lie down in a quiet place where you won't be disturbed.
- Close your eyes and take three deep breaths, inhaling through your nose and exhaling through your mouth.
- Let your muscles soften with each exhale. Feel yourself settling into the present moment.

2. Visualize Your Safe Space

- Picture a place where you feel at peace—a beach, a quiet forest, a cozy cabin, or anywhere that brings you comfort.
- Notice every detail: the colors, the textures, the atmosphere.
- Is the air warm or cool? What time of day is it? Is the sun shining, or are the stars out?

3. Engage Your Senses for Deeper Immersion

- What do you hear? Maybe the soft rustling of leaves, the rhythm of waves, or a crackling fire.
- What do you smell? The salty ocean air, fresh pine trees, or the comforting scent of home.
- What do you feel? The softness of grass beneath you? The warmth of the sun on your skin? Let the sensations anchor you in the moment.

4. Absorb the Feeling of Safety and Comfort

- Take a moment to breathe deeply and absorb the sense of safety.
- If any tension lingers in your body, imagine it melting away into the ground beneath you.
- Let this safe space fill you with calm, warmth, and reassurance.

5. Return to the Present with a Sense of Peace

- tay in your safe space for as long as you need.
- When you're ready, take three deep breaths and gently wiggle your fingers and toes.
- Open your eyes, knowing that this safe place is always within you—accessible anytime you need it.

📌 Tip: The more you practice, the easier it becomes to access this place during stressful moments. Try setting aside 5 minutes a day to strengthen your connection to your safe space.

Exercise: Resourcing for Emotional Strength

This exercise helps you draw strength from positive memories, connections, and sensory experiences, creating an internal toolkit for self-soothing and resilience.

1. Visualize Connection with a Loved One

- Close your eyes and bring to mind someone who makes you feel loved and supported—a friend, family member, mentor, or even a pet.
- Picture their face, their warmth, their presence. What do they say to comfort you?
- Imagine them offering a hug, holding your hand, or simply being there.
- Feel their encouragement surrounding you, filling you with safety and love.

2. Immerse Yourself in a Favorite Nature Spot

- Picture yourself in a calming natural setting—a forest, a garden, the mountains.
- Notice the colors, the sounds, the movement of the air around you.
- Imagine breathing in the pure, fresh air, filling your lungs with peace.

- Let this scene ground you, reminding you of nature's quiet, steady presence.

3. Use Music to Anchor Positive Emotions

- Choose a song that brings joy, comfort, or nostalgia.
- Close your eyes and immerse yourself in the melody, the lyrics, the rhythm.
- Let the music transport you to a memory or feeling of happiness.

4. Carry a Physical Anchor of Meaning

- Keep a small photo, object, or keepsake that holds positive meaning for you.
- When feeling overwhelmed, hold it in your hands, noticing its weight and texture.
- Let it remind you of love, strength, and the things that truly matter.

📌 Tip: Resourcing is most effective when practiced regularly. Try using one of these techniques daily, so they become familiar and easy to access when you need them.

Exercise: Floating Clouds Technique

The Floating Clouds exercise helps you detach from intrusive thoughts, viewing them as passing clouds rather than absolute truths. This technique trains your mind to observe thoughts without getting caught up in them.

1. Get Comfortable and Focus on Your Breath

- Find a quiet place to sit or lie down.
- Close your eyes and take three deep breaths, inhaling through your nose and exhaling through your mouth.
- Allow your body to settle, relax, and let go of tension.

2. Imagine a Vast, Open Sky

- Picture a wide, endless sky stretching above you. It is clear, peaceful, and open.
- This sky represents your mind—spacious, free, and unaffected by passing thoughts.

3. See Your Thoughts as Floating Clouds

- As thoughts arise, visualize them as clouds drifting across the sky.
- Some may be small and wispy, others large and heavy.
- Instead of judging the thoughts, simply acknowledge them and let them drift.

4. Watch the Clouds Move Without Holding Onto Them

- Remind yourself: "Thoughts come and go. They do not define me."
- Focus on the sky itself—calm, vast, and always present beneath the passing clouds.
- Each time a thought arises, observe it, let it go, and return to the sky.

5. Return to the Present with Lightness

- Take a deep breath, feeling lighter and more at ease.
- When ready, wiggle your fingers and toes, bringing awareness back to the room.
- Open your eyes and carry this sense of detachment and peace with you.

📌 Tip: The more you practice, the easier it becomes to observe thoughts rather than be consumed by them.

CHAPTER 3
MINDFULNESS-BASED SOMATIC PRACTICES

Mindfulness-based somatic practices combine the principles of mindfulness with body-focused techniques, enhancing awareness of physical sensations and mental states. Mindfulness involves paying attention to the present moment without judgment. When integrated with somatic therapy, it allows you to observe and connect with the physical sensations that accompany emotions, thoughts, and trauma responses. This approach deepens self-awareness and helps identify patterns that affect your well-being.

In a mindfulness-based somatic practice, you bring your attention to different parts of the body, noticing sensations such as tension, warmth, or pressure. By staying present with these sensations, you create a space to explore emotions and experiences stored in the body. This process helps you become more aware of how your body responds to stress, anxiety, and other emotional states, and it gives you the tools to manage these responses in real-time.

This integration of mindfulness and somatic therapy is beneficial for grounding and calming the nervous system. When you focus on the breath or a specific body part, you anchor yourself in the present, reducing the influence of intrusive thoughts or overwhelming emotions. Over time, practicing mindfulness with somatic techniques increases emotional resilience and promotes self-regulation.

These practices are effective for addressing chronic stress, trauma, and emotional dysregulation. They build your capacity to stay with discomfort without becoming overwhelmed, leading to a greater sense of balance and inner calm. By regularly engaging in mindfulness-based somatic exercises, you can enhance your connection with your body, improve emotional awareness, and cultivate a state of relaxation and presence.

Exercise: Breath-Focused Body Wisdom Meditation

The Breath-Focused Body Wisdom Meditation is a powerful practice designed to connect you deeply with your body and the sensations it holds. This meditation uses the breath as an anchor, guiding you to explore and listen to the wisdom of your body. Through this practice, you cultivate awareness of physical sensations, emotions, and the messages your body communicates, promoting a sense of balance and self-compassion.

Follow the steps below to engage in this meditation.

1: Find a Quiet and Comfortable Space

Begin by finding a quiet, comfortable space where you can sit or lie down without interruptions. Choose a posture that allows your spine to be straight but relaxed. You may sit cross-legged on the floor or in a chair with your feet flat on the ground, or you may lie down if that feels supportive. Close your eyes gently or keep a soft gaze to minimize distractions. Take a moment to settle into your position, noticing the support of the surface beneath you.

2: Connect with Your Breath

Once you are settled, bring your attention to your breath. Inhale deeply through your nose, filling your lungs, and then exhale slowly through your mouth. Focus on the sensation of the breath as it enters and leaves your body. Notice the rise and fall of your chest and the expansion and contraction of your abdomen. Allow the breath to be natural, without trying to control or change it. The breath serves as an anchor, helping you stay connected to the present moment.

3: Begin a Body Scan

With your breath as your guide, begin to shift your attention to different areas of your body. Start at the top of your head, noticing any sensations, such as tension, warmth, or tingling. As you breathe in, imagine sending your breath to this area, inviting a sense of openness and relaxation. As you exhale, release any tension you might be holding.

Move slowly down your body, scanning your face, neck, and shoulders. Continue breathing into each area, bringing gentle awareness to any sensations. If you encounter a spot of discomfort or tightness, breathe into it with curiosity, not judgment. Notice how these areas respond when you give them attention, and let any tension soften with each exhalation.

4: Explore Emotions and Physical Sensations

As you continue scanning down your body, be aware of any emotions that arise. The body often holds onto emotions like stress, anxiety, or sadness in specific areas, such as the chest or stomach. If you sense heaviness, tightness, or another feeling in a particular place, pause and breathe into that spot. Ask yourself, "What is my body communicating to me?" Allow any emotions or thoughts to come up naturally, and observe them without trying to change or judge them.

This process of tuning into body sensations helps you understand how your body and emotions are interconnected. It encourages you to approach these sensations with a sense of curiosity, inviting the wisdom of your body to reveal itself. Often, the body may respond by releasing tension or offering insights into how you are feeling emotionally.

5: Stay with the Breath and Body Connection

As you move further down your body, maintaining a connection to your breath is essential. This allows you to stay grounded, especially when encountering intense or uncomfortable sensations. If your mind wanders or you feel overwhelmed, gently bring your attention back to your breath. Remind yourself that the breath is always available as a source of stability and calm. It acts as an anchor, keeping you rooted in the present moment.

This mindful breathing not only calms the nervous system but also reinforces your connection to your body, making it easier to process emotions that arise. As you continue down to your hips, legs, and feet, notice how these areas feel and whether they hold any tension. Breathe into each part, acknowledging and appreciating the sensations your body offers.

6: Reflect and Integrate

After scanning through your entire body, take a few moments to sit with the sensations you've noticed. What did your body reveal to you? Were there areas that felt tense or emotions that surfaced? Reflect on the experience without judgment. The goal is not to fix or change anything but to create space for awareness and acceptance. Your body holds wisdom, and by paying attention to it, you strengthen your ability to listen and respond with compassion.

To integrate the practice, place one hand on your chest and the other on your abdomen. Feel the warmth and support of your touch. Take a few deep breaths, imagining each inhale as a wave of calm and each exhale as a release of tension. Let this final moment be one of gratitude for your body and its capacity to guide and support you.

7: Return to the Present Moment

When you are ready, gently bring your awareness back to the room. Notice the sounds around you, the feel of the surface beneath you, and the air on your skin. Slowly open your eyes if they were closed, allowing yourself to reconnect with your surroundings. Take your time transitioning out of the meditation, honoring the experience and any insights or sensations that arose.

8: Journaling or Reflecting

To deepen your connection with the practice, consider journaling about your experience. Write down any physical sensations, emotions, or thoughts that stood out during the meditation. Reflect on how your body responded to your attention and what insights you gained from tuning in. This reflection helps reinforce the practice and integrates the wisdom your body shared.

Practicing this meditation regularly builds a stronger connection between your breath and body, enhancing self-awareness. It helps regulate your nervous system, reduces stress, and increases your ability to stay present with emotions and physical sensations. Over time, this practice supports emotional resilience, allowing you to navigate life's challenges with greater ease and compassion.

Let's look at some journaling prompts for reflection and understand our body better:

1. *Where do I feel tension in my body?*
2. *What emotions am I holding onto right now?*
3. *What emotions am I holding onto now?*
4. *What does my body need at this moment?*
5. *How can I ground in this moment?*
6. *What movement feels natural to me right now?*

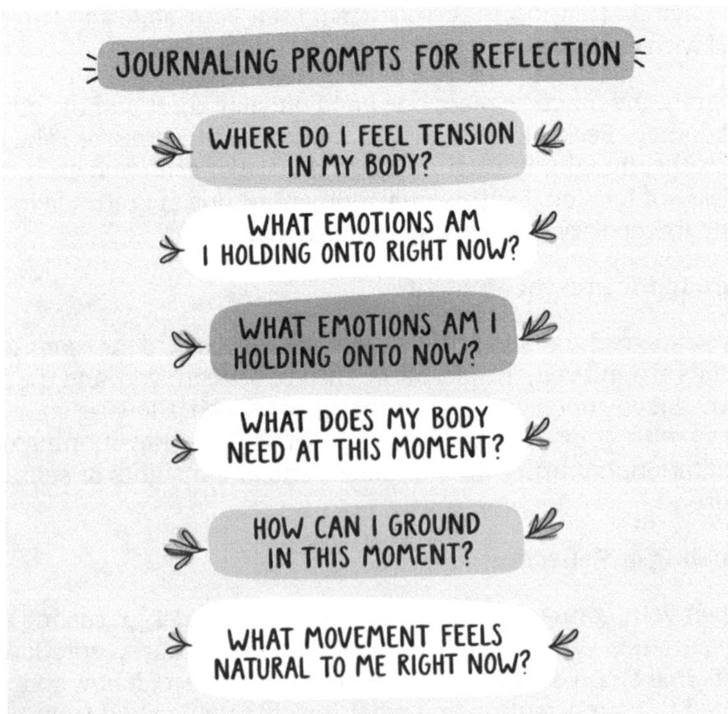

Exercise: Loving-Kindness Meditation

Loving-Kindness Meditation (LKM) is a powerful practice that cultivates feelings of compassion, warmth, and connection toward yourself and others. It is designed to promote a sense of peace, reduce stress, and enhance emotional well-being. This exercise encourages you to send positive energy and good intentions to yourself and the people around you, fostering a state of kindness and empathy. By practicing LKM regularly, you strengthen your capacity for self-compassion and develop a more open-hearted approach to your relationships and life experiences.

1: Find a Comfortable Space

Begin by finding a quiet and comfortable space where you can sit or lie down. Choose a posture that allows your body to relax, with your spine straight but not tense. Close your eyes softly or keep a gentle gaze downward to minimize distractions. Take a few deep breaths to settle into your position, feeling the support of the surface beneath you.

2: Connect with Your Breath

Take a moment to connect with your breath. Inhale deeply through your nose, letting the air fill your lungs, and exhale slowly through your mouth. Focus on the sensation of the breath as it flows in and out, allowing any tension in your body to soften with each exhale. Let your breath be an anchor that keeps you present throughout the meditation.

3: Begin with Self-Compassion

Start by directing loving-kindness toward yourself. Bring your awareness to your heart area and imagine a warm, gentle light radiating from this space. Silently repeat the following phrases to yourself:

"May I be safe."

"May I be happy."

"May I be healthy."

"May I live with ease."

As you say these phrases, try to genuinely feel the meaning behind the words. Imagine yourself enveloped in this light of kindness and compassion, as if you are offering yourself the gift of warmth and care.

4: Extend Loving-Kindness to Others

Once you feel a sense of warmth toward yourself, begin to expand that feeling to others. Start with someone you love, such as a close friend or family member. Picture them in your mind and repeat the same phrases:

"May you be safe."

"May you be happy."

"May you be healthy."

"May you live with ease."

Visualize this person surrounded by the same warm light, receiving your intention of loving-kindness. Allow yourself to genuinely feel the compassion and care you are sending.

5: Extend Loving-Kindness to Neutral People

Next, bring to mind someone you know but do not have strong feelings about, such as an acquaintance or a neighbor. Repeat the same phrases, imagining the light expanding from your heart to theirs. Practicing loving-kindness toward neutral people helps expand your capacity for empathy and kindness beyond your immediate circle.

6: Extend Loving-Kindness to Difficult Individuals

After offering loving-kindness to those you care about and those you feel neutral toward, try extending this practice to someone with whom you may have conflicts or negative feelings. This can be challenging, but it is an important part of cultivating an open heart. Visualize this person and repeat the same phrases:

"May you be safe."

"May you be happy."

"May you be healthy."

"May you live with ease."

Focus on sending them kindness, recognizing that they, too, seek happiness and peace, just as you do.

7: Extend Loving-Kindness to All Beings

Finally, broaden your focus to include all living beings. Imagine the light of loving-kindness spreading out from your heart, touching everyone around you and beyond. Silently repeat:

"May all beings be safe."

"May all beings be happy."

"May all beings be healthy."

"May all beings live with ease."

Envision this warmth and compassion encompassing the entire world, creating a sense of universal connection and kindness.

8: Return to Your Breath

To close the meditation, bring your awareness back to your breath. Notice how you feel in your body and mind. Take a few deep breaths, and when you are ready, gently open your eyes. Take a moment to acknowledge the sense of peace and compassion you have cultivated.

Practicing Loving-Kindness Meditation regularly can help reduce stress, enhance emotional resilience, and improve relationships. It deepens your sense of compassion for yourself and others, promoting a more open and accepting mindset.

Chapter 4
Connecting with the Earth

In today's fast-paced, technology-driven world, many of us feel disconnected from ourselves and our surroundings. Nature-based somatic practices offer a powerful antidote, inviting us to reconnect with our bodies, emotions, and the natural world. These practices harness the healing energy of nature to foster awareness, grounding, and emotional regulation, making them invaluable tools for enhancing well-being.

Nature has a profound impact on our physical and mental health. Studies show that spending time outdoors can reduce stress, improve mood, and enhance cognitive function. Nature-based somatic practices leverage these benefits by encouraging us to engage with our environment mindfully. By immersing ourselves in the sights, sounds, and sensations of the natural world, we can deepen our connection to our bodies and emotions, facilitating healing and self-discovery.

This chapter will explore three transformative exercises that incorporate nature into somatic therapy. Each practice is designed to promote grounding, enhance mindfulness, and facilitate emotional release, allowing you to tap into the restorative qualities of nature. Whether you are walking barefoot on the grass, listening to the sounds of birds, or observing the beauty of a forest, these exercises encourage you to become fully present in your body and environment.

By engaging with nature intentionally, you can cultivate a deeper sense of peace and clarity, making these practices powerful tools for stress management and emotional regulation. As you embark on this journey, be open to the healing potential of the natural world and discover how it can enrich your somatic experience and overall well-being.

Exercise: Nature Walk with Mindfulness

This is a restorative exercise that invites you to immerse yourself in the natural world while enhancing your awareness of your body and surroundings. This practice fosters a deeper connection with nature and promotes relaxation, mindfulness, and emotional balance.

1. Choose a Peaceful Spot

Select an outdoor location that feels calm and inviting, such as a park or forest. Ensure it's a place where you feel safe and comfortable.

2. **Ground Yourself Before You Walk**

Stand still for a moment before beginning your walk. Feel your feet connected to the ground, close your eyes if it feels natural, and take a few deep breaths. As you inhale, visualize energy rising from the earth through your feet, anchoring you in the present moment.

3. **Walk Slowly and Engage Your Senses**

As you walk, slow your pace and notice each step you take. Pay attention to the sound of your footsteps, the colors and textures around you, and the feel of the sun or breeze on your skin. If your mind drifts, gently bring your focus back to these sensations.

Pay attention to how your body feels while walking. Notice any areas of tension or discomfort. Breathe into those areas, allowing your breath to soften any tightness. Acknowledge how your body moves and how it feels in harmony with nature.

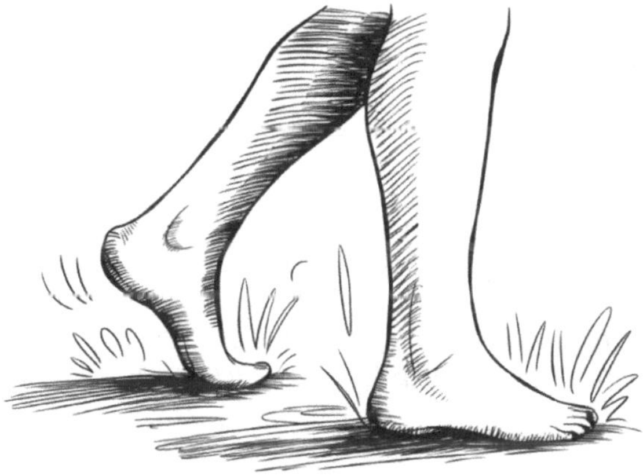

Walk barefoot -
feel the earth beneath you.

4. **Reflect and Breathe to End the Walk**

When your walk is complete, pause for a moment to reflect on what you observed. How did the sounds, smells, and sights affect your emotions? Take a few deep breaths, inhaling the fresh air and releasing any lingering tension, carrying this sense of mindfulness with you into the rest of your day. 5: Tune into Your Body

Exercise: Listening to Nature

This meditative exercise is designed to deepen your connection with the natural world and enhance your sensory awareness. By tuning into the sounds and sensations of nature, you can cultivate a sense of peace, grounding, and emotional balance.

1: Find a Suitable Outdoor Space

Begin by selecting a quiet outdoor space where you can sit or stand comfortably. This could be in a garden, park, or any natural setting that appeals to you. Ensure you feel safe and at ease in your surroundings. Take a moment to settle in, allowing your body to relax and your mind to become present.

2: Ground Yourself

Stand or sit with your feet firmly planted on the ground. Close your eyes if it feels comfortable, and take a few deep breaths. Inhale deeply through your nose, feeling your abdomen rise, and exhale slowly through your mouth. Visualize roots extending from your feet into the earth, anchoring you securely and connecting you with the ground beneath you.

3: Tune into the Sounds

As you settle, begin to focus on the sounds around you. Listen attentively to the natural sounds in your environment—the rustling leaves, chirping birds, flowing water, or distant wind. Allow these sounds to fill your awareness, letting go of any distracting thoughts. If your mind begins to wander, gently bring your focus back to the sounds of nature.

4: Connect with the Elements

Reflect on the four elements—earth, water, air, and fire—and how they manifest in your surroundings. Feel the solidity of the earth beneath you, the coolness of the breeze on your skin, the warmth of the sun, and the sounds of flowing water or rustling leaves. Acknowledge how each element influences your experience and your emotions.

5: Visualize the Elements

As you continue to listen, visualize each element around you. Imagine the earth as a stable foundation, the water as a source of flow and adaptability, the air as a breath of fresh energy, and the fire as warmth and transformation. Allow these visualizations to deepen your connection with nature and enhance your sense of presence.

6: Reflect on Your Feelings

Take a moment to observe any feelings or sensations that arise during this exercise. How do the sounds and elements affect your emotional state? Are there areas of tension or stress that begin to soften? Allow yourself to fully experience these feelings without judgment.

7: Conclude with Gratitude

After spending time listening to nature and connecting with the elements, conclude your practice by expressing gratitude for the natural world. Take a few deep breaths and allow a sense of appreciation to wash over you. When you feel ready, slowly open your eyes and take a moment to notice how your body feels after this experience.

By engaging in the "Listening to Nature" exercise, you cultivate a deeper awareness of your surroundings and enhance your emotional well-being. This practice encourages you to connect with the elements, promoting a sense of grounding and peace that can enrich your daily life.

CHAPTER 5
MOVEMENT-BASED SOMATIC EXERCISES FOR DEPRESSION

Movement is a powerful tool for improving mental health. When you engage in movement, your body releases endorphins. These are chemicals that act as natural painkillers and mood lifters. Exercise stimulates the production of neurotransmitters like serotonin and dopamine. These chemicals help regulate mood and can combat feelings of sadness.

Movement also helps release pent-up tension. When you hold onto stress, it often manifests physically in your body. Engaging in movement allows you to release this tension. This can create a sense of relief and lighten your emotional burden.

Moreover, movement encourages mindfulness. Focusing on your body while moving helps you stay present. This presence can distract from negative thoughts and ruminations associated with depression.

Different types of movement can b e effective. Activities such as walking, yoga, or dancing allow for self-expression and emotional release. As you explore different forms of movement, you may discover what resonates with you. Finding joy in movement can help cultivate a positive mindset and alleviate feelings of depression.

Exercise: Gentle Somatic Stretching: Releasing Tension Held in the Body

Gentle somatic stretching is a powerful practice for releasing tension. It helps you connect with your body

1. Find a Comfortable Space

Settle into a quiet, comfortable space where you can sit or lie down. Make sure you feel safe and relaxed. Close your eyes or soften your gaze to minimize distractions.

2. Begin With Deep Breaths

Take slow, deep breaths. Inhale through your nose, allowing your abdomen to rise, and exhale slowly through your mouth. Feel your body relax as you focus on the flow of your breath.

3. Gentle Stretches for Relaxation

Start with gentle neck stretches by tilting your ear toward your shoulder and holding for a few breaths on each side. Perform shoulder rolls by lifting your shoulders toward your ears as you inhale, and rolling them back as you exhale. Extend your arms overhead, interlace your fingers, and stretch upward. If seated, lean forward into a gentle stretch to release tension in your back and hamstrings. For those comfortable on all fours, try the cat-cow stretch by arching your back as you inhale and rounding it as you exhale.

4. Stay Mindful Throughout the Practice

Remain connected to your breath and body sensations. Pay attention to areas of tension, and with each exhale, imagine releasing it. Allow yourself to relax more deeply with every movement.

5. Conclude The Session

When ready, return to a seated position and take a few final breaths. Reflect on the sensations of relaxation and release, noticing how your body feels after the stretches.

10. Incorporate Stretching into Your Routine

Make these gentle somatic stretches a regular part of your self-care routine. Practicing daily or whenever tension arises promotes relaxation, reduces stress, and supports emotional well-being.

Exercise: Shaking to Release Stagnant Energy

Shaking is an effective practice for releasing stagnant energy. It helps lift your mood and invigorate your body. This exercise encourages freedom of movement and emotional expression.

1. Prepare Your Space and Breath

Find a safe, comfortable space where you can move freely without restriction. Stand with your feet hip-width apart, feeling grounded. Take a few deep breaths, inhaling through your nose and exhaling through your mouth, allowing your body to relax and prepare for movement.

2. Connect with Your Body

Stand still for a moment and tune into your body. Notice any areas of tension, heaviness, or discomfort. Acknowledge your emotional state without judgment, bringing awareness to how you feel in the present moment.

3. Start Shaking and Increase Intensity

Begin shaking your arms gently, letting your hands relax. Gradually introduce movement to your legs and gently shake your head. As the movement becomes more vigorous, allow your body to respond naturally—stomping, bouncing, or swaying as feels right.

4. Incorporate Sound and Sensation

Add sound if it feels comfortable—hum, yell, or laugh to release emotions trapped in your body. Pay attention to the sensations as you shake, visualizing stagnant energy leaving your body. Embrace the spontaneity and freedom of the movement.

5. Slow Down and Reflect

After 5-10 minutes of shaking, gradually slow your movements and return to stillness. Focus on your breath, taking a moment to notice how your body and mood have shifted. Reflect on the experience and consider making shaking a regular practice to release tension and lift your spirits. .

Exercise: Other Movement Practices

Movement practices such as yoga, dance, and Tai Chi offer unique benefits for managing depression. They promote physical and emotional well-being through movement and mindfulness.

Yoga

Yoga combines physical postures, breathwork, and mindfulness. It promotes relaxation and helps release tension. Start with gentle yoga poses like Child's Pose, Cat-Cow, and Downward Dog. Focus on your breath and the sensations in your body. Yoga encourages self-compassion and connection to your body.

Dance

Dance is a creative and expressive form of movement. It allows you to connect with your emotions. Put on your favorite music and move freely. Let your body guide you as you dance. Feel the joy of movement and release any pent-up emotions. Dance is a celebration of your body and spirit.

Tai Chi

Tai Chi is a gentle martial art that emphasizes slow, flowing movements. It promotes relaxation and mindfulness. Begin with simple Tai Chi movements like "Cloud Hands" or "Single Whip." Focus on your breath and the flow of energy in your body. Tai Chi helps cultivate balance and inner peace.

Choose What Resonates with You

Explore different movement practices and see what resonates. You can try a yoga class, a dance workshop, or follow Tai Chi videos online. Find what brings you joy and allows for emotional expression.

Create a Routine

Incorporate these movement practices into your routine. Aim for at least 20-30 minutes of movement several times a week. This regular practice can help improve your mood and reduce feelings of depression.

Stay Present

During these practices, stay present in your body. Pay attention to how you feel physically and emotionally. Allow yourself to fully experience the benefits of movement.

Connect with Others

Consider joining a class or group. Connecting with others can enhance the experience. Share the joy of movement and support each other in your journey.

Reflect on Your Experience

After each session, take a moment to reflect. How did the movement affect your mood? What emotions did you experience? Acknowledge the positive changes you notice in your mental state.

Incorporating movement-based somatic exercises into your routine can significantly alleviate feelings of depression. These practices encourage you to connect with your body, release tension, and express emotions. By embracing movement, you can cultivate a more positive mindset and enhance your emotional well-being.

CHAPTER 6
EMBRACING MUSCLE RELAXATION

Progressive Muscle Relaxation (PMR) is a powerful and effective technique used in somatic therapy to reduce tension, increase body awareness, and promote overall relaxation. Developed by Dr. Edmund Jacobson in the early 20th century, PMR is based on the idea that mental calmness is a natural result of physical relaxation. By focusing on systematically tensing and then relaxing different muscle groups, this practice helps you connect with your body, release accumulated stress, and improve your ability to manage physical and emotional responses.

The core principle of PMR is simple: you intentionally create tension in specific muscles, hold that tension briefly, and then release it slowly. This process allows you to feel the difference between a tense state and a relaxed state, enhancing your awareness of how stress manifests physically. PMR can be done with the whole body, but it can also be adapted into localized techniques focusing on specific areas like the shoulders, jaw, or legs, making it a flexible and accessible practice for different needs.

When practiced regularly, PMR has numerous benefits for both the body and mind. Physiologically, it can reduce muscle stiffness, improve circulation, and lower heart rate. On a mental and emotional level, PMR provides a tool to manage anxiety, stress, and emotional distress. By using the breath in combination with muscle relaxation, the technique engages the parasympathetic nervous system, signaling the body to shift into a state of calm. This makes PMR particularly effective in calming the mind and creating a sense of safety within the body.

PMR also offers a valuable opportunity to deepen your connection with your body, a key component of somatic therapy. Often, we carry tension unknowingly in areas like the shoulders, neck, or jaw. Through PMR, you can tune into these physical sensations and identify the parts of your body where stress tends to accumulate. Over time, this awareness empowers you to respond more effectively to stress, using PMR as a proactive tool to maintain balance and relaxation.

In this chapter, you will explore various PMR exercises tailored to different areas of the body. You will learn how to integrate PMR into your daily routine and practice localized techniques for targeted stress relief. By mastering PMR, you can build a powerful self-care tool that helps you manage physical tension and emotional stress, promoting a state of overall well-being and resilience.

Progressive Muscle Relaxation (PMR) is a simple technique for relaxation.

You can learn it easily. Dr. Edmund Jacobson developed this method in the early 1920s. He published his findings in 1938 in a book called Progressive Relaxation. PMR involves tensing and relaxing 14 different muscle groups in a specific order.

Research

Originally, PMR was used to address anxiety. Over time, research has shown its effectiveness for various conditions. These include tension headaches, migraines, TMJ (temporomandibular joint disorder), neck pain, insomnia, bipolar disorder, anxiety, backaches, and high blood pressure.

The American Academy of Sleep Medicine recognized PMR as an effective non-drug treatment for chronic insomnia in 1999. It helps relax both the body and mind. Many find it useful to practice PMR before bedtime for better sleep.

What It Is

PMR is a two-step practice. It aims to reduce stress and heighten awareness of muscle sensations. In the first step, you create tension in specific muscle groups. You pay attention to what tension feels like in that area. The second step involves releasing that tension and noticing the sensation of relaxation as it dissipates.

You can repeat this process for several muscle groups. By doing so, you deepen your awareness of tension and relaxation. With practice, you can learn to relax your muscles at the first signs of stress. After the session, some areas may still feel tense. You can revisit those areas by repeating the tensing and relaxing steps.

How It Is Taught

You can practice PMR either lying down or sitting. It's crucial not to strain or over-tense your muscles. A little tension is enough to enhance your awareness. If you feel discomfort or cramping, ease up, stop, or skip that muscle group.

Make sure not to hold your breath while tensing your muscles. This can add stress to your body. Instead, synchronize your breathing with your movements. Breathe in while tensing and out while relaxing. This rhythm can enhance your relaxation and calm your mind.

You might find it helpful to say a calming phrase, like "RELAX," as you release each muscle group. Although PMR is simple, it may take several sessions to master. Once you do, you can use a shortened version of the technique. For instance, you can tense only your hands and arms or focus on your forehead, eyes, and jaw.

With practice, you may become proficient enough to focus on just one muscle group to achieve relaxation. Tightening and relaxing a single group while saying "RELAX" can shorten your routine.

Considerations

If you feel very tense, actively tensing your muscles may not help. In this case, consider passive progressive relaxation instead. Always consult with your physician before starting PMR. It may not be suitable if you have serious injuries, muscle spasms, or back issues. Tensing muscles can worsen these conditions.

Exercise: Progressive Muscle Relaxation

1: Find a Comfortable Position

Begin by locating a quiet, comfortable space where you can either sit or lie down. Ensure that your position allows you to relax fully. If it feels comfortable, close your eyes and take a few deep breaths. Inhale deeply through your nose, feeling your abdomen rise, and exhale slowly through your mouth, releasing any tension.

2: Center Yourself

Take a moment to center yourself. Focus on your breath as you inhale and exhale. Notice the sensations in your body as you breathe. Allow yourself to settle into the surface beneath you, feeling supported and safe.

3: Work Through Muscle Groups

Now, focus on the following muscle groups, working through them one at a time:

- Fists: Clench both fists tightly and hold for 5 seconds.

- Biceps: Bend your elbows and tense your bicep muscles for 5 seconds.

- Triceps: Straighten your arms, tensing the muscles in the back of your arms for 5 seconds.

- Forehead: Frown and wrinkle your forehead, holding the tension for 5 seconds.

- Eyes: Close your eyes tightly and hold for 5 seconds.

- Jaw: Gently clench your jaw for 5 seconds.

- Tongue: Press your tongue against the roof of your mouth and hold for 5 seconds.

- Lips: Press your lips together tightly and hold for 5 seconds.

- Neck: Gently press your neck back, then bring your head forward to your chest and hold for 5 seconds.

- Shoulders: Shrug your shoulders up towards your ears, holding for 5 seconds, then let them drop.

- Stomach: Push your stomach out and hold for 5 seconds.

- Lower Back: Gently arch your lower back for 5 seconds.

- Buttocks: Tighten the muscles in your buttocks and hold for 5 seconds.

- Thighs: Lift your legs off the floor and tense your thighs for 5 seconds.

- Calves: Press your toes downward, as if burying them in sand, and hold for 5 seconds.

- Shins and Ankles: Bend your feet toward your head and hold for 5 seconds.

For each muscle group, tense the muscles and hold the tension for five seconds while breathing in. Then, release the tension all at once, paying close attention to how relaxation feels.

4: Repeat as Needed

You can repeat tensing the same muscle group one or two more times, using less tension each time. This practice helps you build awareness of the difference between tension and relaxation.

5: Move to the Next Muscle Group

When you feel comfortable, move to the next muscle group. Remember to breathe steadily throughout the exercise. If you experience pain or discomfort, reduce the tension or skip to the next area.

6: Embrace the Full Experience

After completing the muscle groups, take a moment to appreciate how your body feels now compared to when you started. Spend a few moments in silence, breathing deeply and enjoying the relaxation you have achieved.

7: Gradually Return to the Present

When you're ready, slowly bring your awareness back to the present moment. Wiggle your fingers and toes, take a deep breath, and gently open your eyes. Notice the sense of calm and relaxation throughout your body.

8: Practice Regularly

Incorporate Progressive Muscle Relaxation into your self-care routine, especially during stressful times. Regular practice enhances your awareness of physical tension and promotes relaxation and well-being.

By making PMR a part of your daily life, you empower yourself to manage stress effectively and enhance your emotional health, fostering a stronger connection between your mind and body.

CHAPTER 7
DANCE AND FREE MOVEMENT

Creativity and play are essential components in somatic therapy, offering pathways for emotional expression, physical release, and mental healing. When you incorporate creativity into somatic therapy, you access parts of the brain involved in emotional regulation, imagination, and problem-solving. This can positively impact mental healing by providing an outlet for emotions and fostering resilience. By engaging the body in creative ways, you cultivate self-awareness and develop tools to cope with difficult emotions and trauma, enhancing your overall mental and physical well-being.

Exercise: Freeform Dance and Freedom Movement

1: Setting the Space

Find an open area where you can move freely. Choose music that matches your mood—uplifting, calming, or reflective of your emotional state. If you prefer, dance in silence, focusing solely on bodily sensations. Stand still with your feet hip-width apart and arms relaxed. Take deep breaths, inhaling through your nose and exhaling through your mouth. Feel the ground beneath you, connecting with the earth.

2: Initiating Movement

Begin swaying gently to the music or the rhythm of your breath. Let your body move naturally, following whatever feels good. Pay attention to areas that want to move, like your arms, hips, or legs. Start with small movements, allowing them to grow bigger as you gain comfort. There's no right or wrong way—just follow what feels natural.

3: Exploring Emotions Through Movement

Allow emotions to surface as you move. Notice if your body wants to shake off stress, make energetic motions, or sway gently. If you feel tension, express it through your movements, like shaking your hands or stomping your feet. Let go of self-judgment, and give yourself permission to feel whatever comes up.

Experiment with different ways of moving—stretching, twirling, or moving at various speeds. Explore movements that feel expansive, like reaching upward, and those that feel grounding, like bending down. Pay attention to how these movements influence your mood or energy levels.

4: Slowing Down and Reflecting

After several minutes, begin to slow your movements. Gradually bring yourself back to stillness, feeling the sensations in your body. Take a moment to breathe deeply and reflect on the experience. Notice any shifts in your mood, energy, or body sensations. How did the movement help release emotions or tension?

5: Closing the Practice

To close, place a hand on your heart or abdomen. Take a deep breath, and acknowledge the emotions or sensations that emerged. Thank yourself for taking the time to connect with your body and express freely. Reflect on any insights you gained and how your body feels now compared to when you started.

Exercise: Games of Playful Movement

1: Setting Up the Space

Find a comfortable, open space where you can move freely. If you are practicing with a partner, choose an area where you both have enough room to interact without restriction. Set the intention to engage playfully and explore movements without any specific goals.

2: Exploring Solo Play

If you're practicing alone, start by experimenting with playful, exaggerated movements. Try hopping, skipping, twirling, or pretending to walk through imaginary scenarios like stepping through sticky mud or pretending to be different animals.

Allow yourself to laugh and be open to whatever sensations or emotions arise. This can be an opportunity to shift your mood, release tension, and enjoy a sense of playful freedom.

3: Engaging with a Partner

If you have a partner, try interactive games like 'mirror me,' where one person initiates movements, and the other mirrors them. This game builds connection and trust as you follow each other's lead, moving in harmony. Experiment with different movements—slow and smooth, quick and energetic—while maintaining eye contact.

Another playful option is 'freeze dance.' Turn on music and dance freely. When the music stops, freeze in a funny or exaggerated pose. This playful activity encourages spontaneity and helps break patterns of rigidity, inviting a sense of joy.

4: Reflecting on the Experience

After engaging in playful movement for about 10-15 minutes, pause and check in with your body. Take a few deep breaths, noticing any changes in your energy, mood, or physical sensations. Reflect on how it felt to move without judgment and to explore playfulness. You might notice a sense of lightness, increased energy, or emotional release.

5: Closing the Practice

Conclude the exercise with a moment of stillness. Stand with your feet on the ground, feeling the sensations in your body. Take a deep breath, acknowledging the joy and playfulness you experienced. Appreciate the opportunity to connect with your body in a creative, freeing way.

Games of playful movement help you reconnect with your inner child, breaking the rigidity of stress patterns. By engaging in these exercises, you enhance body awareness, release tension, and cultivate emotional resilience through joyful and expressive movement.

CHAPTER 8
HARNESSING SOUND FOR HEALING

In the realm of somatic therapy, sound healing emerges as a transformative practice that engages the body, mind, and spirit in a profound way. As we navigate our emotional landscapes, the vibrations and frequencies of sound offer a unique avenue for connection and release. This chapter introduces two powerful exercises: using the soothing tones of a singing bowl and the healing properties of music. Both practices serve to calm the nervous system, enhance emotional regulation, and promote a sense of inner peace.

Sound has long been recognized for its therapeutic qualities. From ancient cultures utilizing drums and chants to modern practitioners incorporating sound baths, the resonance of sound waves can stimulate profound shifts within our bodies. By engaging with sound, we can tap into the subconscious, accessing feelings and memories often locked away in the depths of our being. The exercises in this chapter not only provide a means to relax but also create an opportunity for deeper self-exploration and healing.

Exercise: The Voo Sound: Settling the Nervous System

The Voo Sound is a therapeutic technique designed to promote relaxation and grounding. By utilizing vocalization, this exercise can help you settle your nervous system and connect with your body.

1: Create a Safe Space

Begin by finding a quiet, comfortable place where you can practice without interruption. This could be a bathroom, your car, or a peaceful outdoor setting. Ensure that you feel safe and calm, as this technique can be more effective in a tranquil environment.

2: Notice Your State

Take a moment to tune into your current physical and emotional state. Acknowledge any feelings of tension or discomfort in your body and prepare to address them through the Voo Sound.

3: Visualize the Foghorn

Think about the deep, resonating sound made by a foghorn, the horn of a ship. If you're unfamiliar with it, you might want to listen to a sample for reference.

4: Inhale Deeply

Take a deep breath in through your nose, allowing your abdomen to expand as you fill your lungs.

5: Produce the Voo Sound

As you exhale, imitate the foghorn by vocalizing the sound "Voo" in the lowest pitch you can manage. Aim to feel the vibrations resonate through your torso and down to your pelvic floor. It's essential to focus on the depth of the sound rather than the volume; keep it soft if that feels right.

6: Observe Your Body's Response

If you feel a sense of settling or calmness in your body, allow yourself to stay in that space and enjoy the feeling. However, if you notice heightened activation or discomfort, it might be best to pause and choose a different exercise for the time being.

8: Repeat if Beneficial

If the Voo Sound brings a sense of peace, you may repeat it up to three times in one session. Each repetition can deepen the settling experience.

Incorporating the Voo Sound into your self-care routine can effectively promote relaxation and emotional regulation. By connecting with your voice and body, you create a powerful tool for settling your nervous system and enhancing your well-being.

Exercise: Sound Healing with Music

1. Create a Comfortable Space

Begin by finding a quiet and comfortable area where you can sit or lie down without distractions. Adjust the environment to encourage relaxation—dim the lights, close the door, or use a blanket or cushion for added comfort. Make sure you feel at ease in this space, as it sets the tone for your sound healing session. A peaceful setting allows your mind and body to fully engage with the sounds, helping you unwind and enter a state of calm.

2. Begin the Sound and Focus on It

Select a sound source that resonates with you, such as soothing instrumental music, nature sounds, or a singing bowl. Play the music at a gentle volume or, if using a singing bowl, softly strike it to create a vibration. As the sound fills the space, bring your attention to it—notice the rhythm, vibrations, and tones. Let the sound wash over you, inviting relaxation and stillness. Focus on how the sound resonates with your surroundings and within your body, helping to release tension and foster mindfulness.

3. Tune Into Your Body and Transition Back

While listening to the sound, gently check in with your body. Notice any areas of tension or discomfort, and visualize the vibrations flowing through you, releasing stress and encouraging relaxation. If it feels right, allow your body to respond naturally with soft movements like stretching or swaying. When you feel ready to conclude the session, slowly transition back to the present moment by wiggling your fingers and toes. Take a few deep breaths, noticing how the sound has affected your mood and body. Embrace the calm it has created, and consider making sound healing a regular part of your self-care routine for ongoing emotional well-being.

BOOK 3

Coping Skills

CHAPTER 1
INTRODUCTION TO SOMATIC THERAPY FOR MENTAL HEALTH

Somatic therapy focuses on the connection between the mind and body. It recognizes that emotions and psychological issues manifest physically.

In this therapy, you engage with your body's sensations, movements, and experiences. This practice allows you to reconnect with your physical self and understand how emotions influence your body.

By doing so, you gain insight into patterns that may contribute to mental health challenges. Instead of solely addressing thoughts and feelings, somatic therapy invites you to explore the physical sensations linked to those experiences. This holistic approach can lead to greater emotional regulation and resilience, helping you cope with life's challenges more effectively.

Understanding the Mind-Body Connection

The mind-body connection is a fundamental concept in somatic therapy. Your thoughts and emotions directly impact your physical health. When you experience stress or trauma, your body often responds with tension, pain, or discomfort. These physical manifestations can be signals of unresolved emotional issues.

For instance, anxiety may present as tightness in your chest or shallow breathing. Similarly, feelings of sadness might be felt as heaviness in your limbs. Recognizing these connections helps you understand how your mental state influences your physical well-being. Your body holds memories of past experiences, both positive and negative. Somatic therapy invites you to explore these memories through physical sensations, allowing for emotional release and healing.

When you feel overwhelmed, your body may go into a fight-or-flight response, triggering physical symptoms like increased heart rate or sweating. This reaction is natural, but chronic stress can lead to long-term health problems, including fatigue, digestive issues, and weakened immunity. By paying attention to these bodily sensations, you can gain valuable insights into your emotional state.

Understanding the mind-body connection empowers you to take an active role in your healing process. You learn to listen to your body's signals and respond to them with care and compassion. This awareness fosters self-acceptance and encourages you to cultivate a supportive relationship with your body. In this way, somatic therapy can enhance your overall mental health and well-being.

Exercise: Body Scan for Mental Awareness

The body scan is a foundational somatic therapy exercise designed to deepen mindfulness and increase awareness of physical sensations that mirror mental states. This practice enables a connection with the body, offering insight into how emotions manifest physically.

1. Find a Comfortable Position

Begin in a quiet, comfortable space where you can sit or lie down undisturbed. Close your eyes or soften your gaze, and take deep breaths, inhaling through your nose and exhaling through your mouth. Let each breath bring relaxation to your body.

2. Focus on Your Breath

Shift your attention to the rhythm of your breathing, noticing the inhale and exhale. Allow your breath to guide you into relaxation, feeling your body become heavier and more grounded with each breath. Release any tension as you exhale.

3. Start Scanning from Head to Toe

Begin at the top of your head, observing any sensations—warmth, tension, or tingling—without judgment. Slowly direct your focus down to your forehead, jaw, and neck, paying attention to areas of tightness or discomfort. Progress down through your shoulders, chest, and abdomen. Notice if any physical sensations, like tightness, correlate with emotions such as anxiety or fear, and allow yourself to feel them fully.

4. Acknowledge Your Arms, Legs, and Feet

Move your focus to your arms and hands, noting sensations in your wrists and fingers. Then, direct your awareness to your legs and feet, observing any areas of tension or relaxation. Consider what these sensations may signify about your emotional state.

5. Reflect on the Experience

Once the scan is complete, take a moment to reflect on what you noticed. Did any emotions arise? Journal your observations to deepen your understanding of the mind-body connection.

6. Practice Regularly

Aim to integrate the body scan into your routine, practicing daily or several times a week. Regular practice enhances awareness of your body's signals, fostering a healthier relationship between your mind and body. Over time, this exercise can be a powerful tool in your somatic therapy journey, promoting emotional regulation and overall mental well-being.

CHAPTER 2
GROUNDING TECHNIQUES FOR ANXIETY AND STRESS

Managing anxiety and stress can be challenging, but somatic techniques offer effective tools to help you find calm and stability. These practices focus on connecting your mind and body, allowing you to process emotions and physical sensations. Below are two powerful exercises designed to ground you in the present moment and promote a sense of safety and tranquility.

Exercise: 5-4-3-2-1 Grounding Method

The 5-4-3-2-1 grounding method is a simple yet effective exercise that uses your senses to bring awareness to the present. This technique can help you reduce feelings of anxiety and stress by shifting your focus from overwhelming thoughts to your immediate surroundings.

1: Find a Comfortable Position

Begin by finding a comfortable sitting or standing position. Ensure you are in a quiet space where you can focus. Take a few deep breaths, inhaling through your nose and exhaling through your mouth. Allow your body to relax.

2: Engage Your Senses

Now, start the 5-4-3-2-1 exercise by engaging your senses one at a time:

5 Things You Can See: Look around you and identify five things you can see. They can be anything in your environment—colors, shapes, or objects. For example, notice the texture of a wall or the pattern of a rug.

4 Things You Can Feel: Shift your attention to your body. Notice four things you can feel. This could be the chair supporting you, the ground beneath your feet, the fabric of your clothing, or even the temperature of the air on your skin

FEEL THE GROUND BENEATH YOUR FEET.

3 Things You Can Hear: Close your eyes if you feel comfortable and listen closely. Identify three sounds around you. These can be soft, like the rustle of leaves, or louder, like traffic or music. Focus on how each sound resonates in your space.

2 Things You Can Smell: Pay attention to your sense of smell. Identify two scents in your environment. If you can't smell anything right now, think of your favorite scents, like fresh coffee or blooming flowers. Visualizing these smells can help bring a sense of comfort.

1 Thing You Can Taste: Finally, focus on one thing you can taste. This could be the aftertaste of a meal, a sip of water, or even the taste of your breath. If you can't taste anything right now, take a moment to sip water or chew a piece of gum to engage this sense.

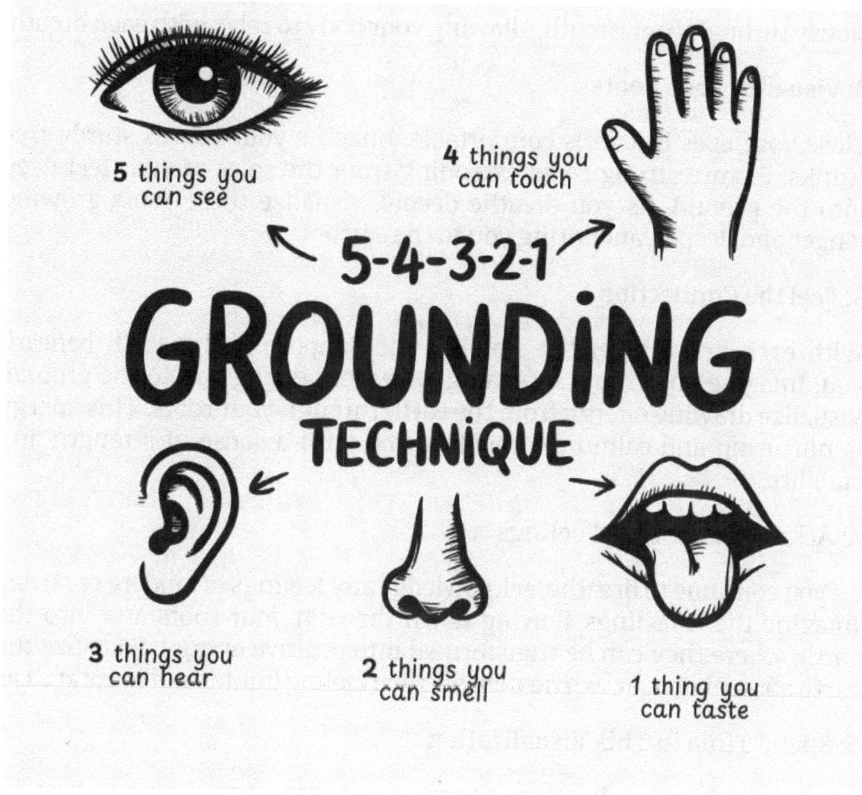

3: Reflect on Your Experience

After completing the 5-4-3-2-1 exercise, take a few moments to notice how you feel. Has your anxiety decreased? Are you more present in the moment? Reflect on your experience in a journal if you'd like.

4: Practice Regularly

Incorporate the 5-4-3-2-1 grounding method into your daily routine or whenever you feel overwhelmed. This practice can help you stay anchored in the present, reducing anxiety and stress as you cultivate a deeper awareness of your surroundings.

Exercise: Tree Root Visualization

The Tree Root Visualization exercise is a powerful imagery technique that helps you feel grounded and stable. By envisioning roots extending from your feet into the earth, you can cultivate a sense of calm and security.

1: Find a Comfortable Position

Begin by sitting or standing in a quiet, comfortable space. Take a few deep breaths to center yourself. Inhale deeply through your nose and exhale slowly through your mouth, allowing your body to relax with each breath.

2: Visualize Your Roots

Close your eyes if it feels comfortable. Imagine your feet as sturdy tree trunks. Picture strong roots extending from the soles of your feet deep into the ground. As you breathe deeply, visualize these roots growing longer and deeper, anchoring you to the earth.

3: Feel the Connection

With each breath, feel the stability and support of the earth beneath you. Imagine your roots spreading wide, connecting you to the ground. Visualize drawing energy from the earth through your roots. This energy is nurturing and calming, providing you with a sense of strength and stability.

4: Acknowledge Your Feelings

As you continue to breathe, acknowledge any feelings of anxiety or stress. Imagine these feelings flowing down through your roots and into the earth, where they can be transformed into positive energy. Visualize the earth absorbing your worries, leaving you feeling lighter and more at ease.

5: Spend Time in This Visualization

Remain in this visualization for several minutes, continuing to breathe deeply and allow yourself to connect with the earth. Feel the support and stability that the roots provide. If your mind wanders, gently bring your focus back to your roots and the sensations in your body.

6: Gradually Return to the Present

When you're ready, slowly bring your awareness back to the present moment. Wiggle your fingers and toes, feeling the connection to the ground beneath you. Take a deep breath and open your eyes, noticing how you feel after this exercise.

7: Practice Regularly

Make Tree Root Visualization a part of your self-care routine, especially when you feel anxious or stressed. This practice can help you cultivate a sense of calm and grounding, allowing you to navigate challenging emotions with greater ease.

By incorporating these somatic techniques into your daily life, you can effectively manage anxiety and stress. Engaging your senses and visualizing stability through grounding exercises fosters a deeper connection between your mind and body, promoting overall well-being.

Exercise: Grounding Techniques for Calm and Stability

Grounding exercises can help you feel present and connected, providing comfort during stressful moments. These practices use touch and sensory focus to bring you back to the here and now.

1. Run Cool or Warm Water Over Your Hands

Place your hands under cool or warm running water, focusing on the temperature and sensation. Notice how the water soothes and refreshes you, helping you center your attention and feel grounded.

2. Give Yourself a Gentle Hug

Wrap your arms around yourself in a gentle hug. Feel the warmth and pressure of your arms, creating a comforting, self-soothing effect that brings a sense of safety and grounding.

3. Wrap in a Soft Blanket or Grounding Sheet

Use a soft blanket or grounding sheet to wrap yourself. The physical warmth provides comfort, while grounding sheets, with conductive materials like carbon or silver, help connect you to the earth's energy for a deeper sense of calm.

4. Squeeze a Stress Ball

Hold a stress ball and squeeze it slowly, focusing on the pressure and release. Concentrating on this repetitive action can help redirect your attention, relieving tension and bringing you back to the present.

CHAPTER 3
SELF-REGULATION PRACTICES FOR TRAUMA

Trauma impacts the body in deep and lasting ways. It triggers responses that can persist long after the traumatic event has passed. When you experience trauma, your body may go into a state of hyperarousal (fight or flight) or hypoarousal (freeze or collapse). These responses are the body's natural way of protecting itself, but they can become stuck, leading to chronic stress or numbness. Trauma can also manifest as physical symptoms like muscle tension, digestive issues, or headaches.

Understanding these bodily responses is the first step toward healing. By becoming aware of how trauma shows up in your body, you can begin to use self-regulation practices. These practices help you release stored tension and regain a sense of safety. They focus on grounding and stabilizing your nervous system, making it possible to move from a state of survival to one of presence and calm.

Exercise: EMDR-Inspired Bilateral Stimulation for Trauma Processing

EMDR (Eye Movement Desensitization and Reprocessing) uses bilateral stimulation to help process traumatic memories. Alternating movements engage both sides of the brain, supporting emotional regulation and integrating distressing memories. While formal EMDR requires a trained therapist, you can practice a simplified version at home using bilateral movements like tapping. This practice aids in emotional regulation, trauma processing, and fostering stability.

1. Prepare Your Space and Ground Yourself

Find a quiet, comfortable place where you feel safe and supported, either sitting or lying down with your feet grounded. Begin with deep breaths—inhaling through your nose, exhaling through your mouth—to calm your nervous system and prepare for the exercise.

2. Select a Bilateral Movement

Engage in a rhythmic movement that alternates between both sides of your body. Some options include tapping your hands on your thighs, passing a small object like a pillow between hands, or crossing your arms to tap your shoulders. Maintain a gentle, steady rhythm.

3. Visualize a Safe Space

While performing the bilateral movement, visualize a calming image or memory, such as a peaceful beach or quiet forest. Focus on sensory details—the sounds, sights, and sensations—deepening your sense of safety and grounding.

4. Tune Into Sensations and Emotions

As you continue, notice any physical sensations, like tension or warmth, and any emotions that arise, such as anxiety or sadness. Stay present, using your movement and breath to stay grounded. If emotions become overwhelming, pause and place your hand on your chest to feel the warmth and reassurance of your touch.

5. Return to the Present Moment

After several minutes, slow the movement and take deep breaths. Gradually open your eyes, reconnecting with your surroundings. Notice the details of the room, sounds, and the feeling of your feet on the ground. This transition helps you return fully to the present, maintaining a sense of calm and control.

Practice and Integration

With regular practice, this exercise builds resilience and supports trauma processing by helping your body stay calm and present, even when difficult emotions arise. This consistent practice fosters emotional regulation, healing, and a sense of safety within yourself..

Exercise: How to Practice Bilateral Stimulation for Trauma Processing

This exercise is designed to help you engage in a self-guided form of bilateral stimulation, using gentle movements to help your body and brain work together. Follow the steps below to safely and effectively engage in this practice.

1: Create a Safe and Comfortable Environment

Before starting the exercise, find a quiet space where you feel safe and comfortable. This is important as the process may bring up emotions or memories related to trauma. Make sure the environment feels secure, with minimal distractions. Sit comfortably in a chair with your feet flat on the ground, or lie down if that feels more supportive for you. Have a soft object nearby, like a ball or a pillow, that you can use for tapping.

Take a few moments to settle into your space. Notice your surroundings and focus on anything that feels comforting, like the support of the chair or the softness of a blanket. These small details help establish a sense of safety, which is crucial for engaging with trauma-related work.

2: Begin with Grounding Breaths

Start the exercise with grounding breaths to center yourself. Close your eyes if it feels comfortable, and take a deep breath in through your nose, filling your lungs completely. Hold for a moment, then exhale slowly through your mouth. Repeat this process for several breaths, paying attention to the rise and fall of your chest or the feeling of the air passing through your nose and mouth.

Grounding breaths are essential because they help you connect with your body and the present moment. When working with trauma, it is important to maintain awareness of your breath as it serves as an anchor if emotions become overwhelming. Breathing deeply and slowly calms your nervous system, allowing you to approach the next steps with a sense of stability.

3: Choose a Bilateral Movement

Bilateral stimulation involves engaging both sides of the body alternately. For this exercise, you can choose from several types of movements:

Tapping: Tap your hands on your thighs alternately, left and right. This rhythmic tapping engages both sides of your body.

Passing an Object: Use a small object like a ball or pillow, and pass it from one hand to the other, moving your hands across your body.

Butterfly Taps: Cross your arms over your chest, placing your hands on opposite shoulders. Gently tap one shoulder at a time, alternating left and right.

Choose the movement that feels most comfortable and natural for you. The goal is to create a steady, rhythmic pattern that you can maintain throughout the exercise. Start slowly and gently, focusing on the movement and the rhythm.

4: Focus on a Calming Image or Memory

As you engage in the bilateral movement, bring to mind a calming image, memory, or place where you feel safe and relaxed. This could be a beach, a forest, a quiet room, or any other space that brings you comfort. Try to imagine this scene vividly, engaging as many senses as possible. What do you see? What sounds are present? Can you feel the warmth of the sun or the coolness of the breeze?

By focusing on a soothing image, you create a sense of safety that helps you stay grounded while working with difficult emotions or memories. The image acts as a mental anchor, reducing the intensity of distress and allowing you to engage with the exercise more fully.

5: Observe the Movement of Thoughts

As you engage in the exercise, you might notice thoughts or memories entering your mind. This is normal, especially when working with trauma. Instead of getting caught up in the thoughts, visualize them as if they are floating on a stream or drifting by like clouds in the sky. Remind yourself that these thoughts are temporary. They come and go, just like clouds.

If a specific memory or image feels overwhelming, gently bring your focus back to your breath or the safe space you visualized earlier. You can pause the bilateral movement and place your hands over your heart, feeling the warmth and support of your touch. When you feel ready, return to the movement, using it to regulate and stabilize your emotions.

6: Return to the Present Moment

When you feel ready to end the exercise, gradually slow down the bilateral movement. Pause, place your hands on your lap or over your heart, and take a few deep breaths. Gently bring your attention back to your surroundings, noticing the sounds, smells, and objects around you. Open your eyes slowly if they have been closed, and allow yourself to reconnect with the present moment.

Take a moment to reflect on how you feel. You may notice a sense of calm, relief, or lightness. Alternatively, you may still feel emotions or sensations present in your body. Whatever you notice, acknowledge it with compassion. Remember that this practice is about building awareness and capacity, and it's okay to feel whatever is present.

Regular practice of bilateral stimulation helps your body learn to process trauma in manageable ways. Over time, it enhances your ability to regulate emotions, stay present, and reduce the intensity of trauma responses. Practicing in short, consistent sessions builds resilience and creates a sense of safety in your body.

CHAPTER 4
ARTISTIC EXPRESSION AND JOURNALING

Artistic expression serves as a powerful tool in somatic therapy, enabling individuals to explore and process emotions in a creative and embodied way. This approach recognizes that the body holds memories and feelings that may be difficult to articulate verbally. By engaging in artistic activities such as drawing, painting, or sculpting, you can access deeper layers of your emotional landscape, allowing for healing and self-discovery.

Exercise: Journaling as Somatic Therapy: Connecting Mind and Body Through Writing

Journaling is a powerful tool in somatic therapy, enabling individuals to explore their emotions and bodily sensations through the written word. This practice fosters self-reflection and emotional processing, allowing you to connect with your inner self in a meaningful way.

1: Create a Safe Space

Begin by finding a quiet and comfortable space where you can write without distractions. Settle into a chair or find a cozy spot on the floor. Gather your journaling materials, such as a notebook and pen. Take a few deep breaths to prepare yourself for this reflective practice. Inhale deeply through your nose, allowing your abdomen to expand, and exhale slowly through your mouth, letting go of any tension.

2: Center Yourself

Take a moment to ground yourself in the present. Close your eyes if it feels comfortable and focus on your breath. Feel the air entering your body and the gentle release as you breathe out. Visualize your breath as a calming wave that washes over you, allowing your body to relax into the surface beneath you.

3: Tune into Your Body

Before you begin writing, bring your awareness to your body. Notice any areas of tension or discomfort. Are there feelings you've been holding onto? Take a moment to acknowledge these sensations without judgment. This is an opportunity to connect with your physical self, laying the groundwork for your journaling.

4: Start Writing

Begin to write freely about your thoughts and emotions. Let your pen flow without censoring yourself. You might start with how you feel in your body at that moment—are there tight areas, or do you feel relaxed? Describe these sensations in detail, allowing your writing to mirror your bodily experience.

5: Explore Emotions

As you write, delve into any emotions that arise. If you feel anxiety, describe how it manifests physically. Does it feel like a knot in your stomach or tension in your shoulders? By expressing these feelings on paper, you can gain insight into how they affect you both mentally and physically.

6: Gradually Return to the Present

When you're ready, slowly bring your awareness back to your surroundings. Wiggle your fingers and toes, and take a deep breath. Open your eyes, noticing any changes in your body or mind after this exercise.

7: Practice Regularly

Incorporate journaling into your self-care routine, especially during times of stress or emotional turmoil. Regular practice helps deepen your awareness of your thoughts, emotions, and physical sensations, empowering you to navigate life's challenges with greater ease.

By integrating journaling as a somatic therapy into your daily life, you foster a stronger connection between your mind and body. This practice allows for emotional exploration and healing, promoting overall well-being and a deeper understanding of your inner self.

Exercise: Artistic Expression as Somatic Therapy: Exploring Emotions Through Creativity

Artistic expression is a transformative exercise in somatic therapy that allows individuals to explore and communicate their emotions through creative outlets such as drawing, painting, or sculpting. This practice engages both the mind and body, fostering a deeper understanding of one's feelings and experiences.

1: Create a Safe Space

Begin by finding a quiet and comfortable space where you can create without interruptions. Gather your artistic materials, such as paper, paints, markers, or clay. Settle into your workspace and take a few deep breaths to prepare yourself for this expressive journey. Inhale deeply through your nose, allowing your abdomen to rise, and exhale slowly through your mouth, letting go of any tension.

2: Center Yourself

Take a moment to center yourself in the present moment. Close your eyes if it feels comfortable and focus on your breath. Feel the air entering your body and the gentle release as you breathe out. Visualize each breath as a wave of calm washing over you, creating a supportive environment for your creative process.

3: Tune into Your Emotions

Before you begin creating, bring your awareness to your emotions. What feelings are present for you right now? Take a moment to acknowledge these emotions without judgment. Consider how they manifest in your body. Are there areas of tension or discomfort? Allow these sensations to form your artistic expression.

4: Begin Creating

Start your artistic process by letting your intuition guide you. Use colors, shapes, and forms that resonate with your current emotional state. Don't worry about creating a "perfect" piece of art; instead, focus on expressing your feelings freely. Allow your brush or hands to move in response to your emotions, embodying what you are experiencing.

5: Explore Your Body's Movement

As you create, notice how your body moves. The physical act of drawing, painting, or molding clay can evoke different sensations. Pay attention to how your body feels in relation to your art. Are you tensing up, or do you feel a sense of release? Embrace these sensations, allowing your movements to reflect your emotional journey.

6: Reflect on Your Creation

After you've spent some time creating, take a moment to step back and observe your artwork. What does it represent for you? Consider the colors, shapes, and textures you used. Reflect on how this piece encapsulates your emotions and physical sensations. Allow yourself to appreciate the process of creation and the insights it offers.

7: Embrace the Full Experience

Acknowledge the overall experience of artistic expression. Notice how your body feels after creating. Are there shifts in your emotional state or physical sensations? Spend a few moments in silence, allowing your thoughts to settle. Appreciate the release and clarity that can come from expressing yourself artistically.

8: Gradually Return to the Present

When you're ready, slowly bring your awareness back to your surroundings. Wiggle your fingers and toes, and take a deep breath. Open your eyes, noticing how you feel after this exercise. Reflect on the emotional journey you've taken through your art.

9: Practice Regularly

Incorporate artistic expression into your self-care routine, especially during times of emotional distress. Regular practice helps deepen your emotional awareness and fosters a sense of empowerment through creativity.

By integrating artistic expression as a somatic therapy into your daily life, you nurture a stronger connection between your mind and body. This practice allows for emotional exploration and healing, promoting overall well-being and providing a unique outlet for self-discovery.

CHAPTER 5
NOURISHING THE MIND AND BODY

Mindful eating is a practice that encourages individuals to be fully present during meals, engaging their senses and enhancing their relationship with food. It involves paying attention to the experience of eating—how food looks, smells, tastes, and feels—while also tuning into hunger and satiety cues. This approach contrasts with habitual or distracted eating, where one may eat mindlessly, often leading to overeating or poor food choices.

The importance of mindful eating in the context of mental health cannot be overstated. In today's fast-paced world, many individuals struggle with stress, anxiety, and emotional eating. By practicing mindfulness during meals, individuals can cultivate a greater awareness of their eating habits and emotional triggers. This awareness fosters healthier relationships with food, reducing the tendency to eat in response to emotions rather than hunger. Mindful eating can help individuals recognize cravings, differentiate between emotional and physical hunger, and promote a more balanced approach to nutrition.

Research indicates that mindful eating can lead to improved mental health outcomes. It encourages individuals to savor their food, which enhances the eating experience and promotes gratitude. This practice can also reduce stress and anxiety levels by creating a calming ritual around meals. Additionally, by fostering a positive relationship with food, individuals may experience decreased symptoms of depression and anxiety, as well as improved body image and self-esteem.

Incorporating mindful eating into daily life is a simple yet effective way to enhance overall well-being. It encourages individuals to slow down, appreciate their meals, and nourish both their bodies and minds. By developing this practice, individuals can transform their eating habits, support their mental health, and foster a deeper connection with themselves and their food.

Exercise: Mindful Eating Practice

Mindful Eating is an essential practice that encourages you to be fully present during meals. By engaging with your food using all your senses, you can enhance your eating experience, promote healthier habits, and cultivate a greater awareness of hunger and satiety cues.

1: Choose Your Food

Select a meal or snack that you want to practice mindful eating with. It can be anything from a piece of fruit to a full meal. Ensure it's something you enjoy, as this will enhance your experience.

2: Create a Calm Environment

Find a quiet space where you can eat without distractions. Turn off your phone, television, or any other distractions. Sit at a table and place your food in front of you, allowing yourself to focus solely on the meal.

3: Observe Your Food

Take a moment to observe your food. Notice its colors, shapes, and textures. What do you see? How does it make you feel? Engaging your senses at this stage prepares you for a more mindful experience.

4: Smell Your Food

Before you take a bite, bring your food close to your nose and take a few deep breaths. Notice the aromas and how they make you feel. Allow the scents to enhance your anticipation for the meal.

5: Take a Small Bite

When you're ready, take a small bite of your food. Chew slowly and intentionally, allowing the flavors to unfold. Pay attention to the taste and texture as you chew, savoring every moment.

6: Check in with Your Body

As you eat, periodically pause to check in with your body. Are you feeling full? Are you still hungry? Notice any sensations, cravings, or feelings that arise as you eat, allowing yourself to become aware of your body's signals.

7: Reflect on the Experience

After finishing your meal, take a moment to reflect on the experience. How did it feel to eat mindfully? Did you notice any changes in your hunger levels or emotional state? Consider journaling about your experience if it resonates with you.

8: Practice Regularly

Incorporate mindful eating into your routine by choosing at least one meal each day to practice. Regular practice will help you cultivate a deeper awareness of your eating habits and promote a healthier relationship with food.

By engaging in mindful eating, you empower yourself to transform your relationship with food. This practice encourages emotional awareness and promotes healthier eating habits, ultimately fostering a greater sense of well-being and connection to your body.

Exercise: The Gratitude Meal

The Gratitude Meal is a mindful eating exercise designed to enhance your appreciation for food and cultivate a sense of gratitude for the nourishment it provides. This practice allows you to connect with your meal on a deeper level, promoting mindfulness and positive emotions.

1: Choose Your Meal

Select a meal you enjoy or one that you would like to appreciate more. This can be breakfast, lunch, or dinner. Aim for a balanced meal that includes a variety of flavors and textures to enhance the experience.

2: Prepare Your Space

Set the table for your meal, creating a pleasant environment. Use a clean plate, utensils, and any decorative items you enjoy. Ensure you have minimal distractions, allowing you to focus entirely on the meal.

3: Reflect on Your Food's Journey

Before you begin eating, take a moment to reflect on the journey of your food. Consider where it came from, who grew or prepared it, and the effort involved in bringing it to your table. Acknowledge the interconnectedness of all elements involved in your meal.

4: Begin with a Moment of Gratitude

Take a deep breath and express gratitude for your meal. You can do this silently or verbally. Acknowledge the nourishment it will provide for your body and mind, allowing this sense of gratitude to fill you.

5: Engage Your Senses

As you start your meal, engage your senses fully. Notice the colors, textures, and aromas of your food. Pay attention to how the food looks on your plate and how it makes you feel. Allow your senses to guide your experience.

6: Take Your Time

Eat slowly, savoring each bite. Chew your food thoroughly and pay attention to the flavors and textures. Allow yourself to enjoy the experience without rushing. If you find yourself eating quickly, gently remind yourself to slow down.

7: Pause and Reflect

Throughout your meal, take pauses to reflect on how you're feeling.

Check in with your body's hunger and fullness cues. Are you still enjoying the meal? Do you feel satisfied? Allow these reflections to enhance your awareness.

8: Conclude with Appreciation

Once you finish your meal, take a moment to reflect on the entire experience. Consider how the meal nourished you both physically and emotionally. Express gratitude for the food, the process, and the moment you've taken to connect with it.

By practicing the Gratitude Meal, you can deepen your appreciation for food and promote a more mindful approach to eating. This exercise encourages emotional awareness and nurtures a positive relationship with food, ultimately enhancing your overall well-being and mental health.

CHAPTER 6
BREATHWORK FOR EMOTIONAL REGULATION

The body plays a vital role in emotional processing. Emotions are physical experiences. When you feel angry or anxious, your body reacts. You might feel tightness in your chest or tension in your shoulders. These sensations signal your emotional state.

Somatic techniques encourage self-awareness. They enhance your emotional intelligence. You learn to express feelings safely and constructively. This fosters a better understanding of your emotions. It empowers you to handle challenging situations with confidence.

Exercise: Techniques for Recognizing and Expressing Emotions

Recognizing and expressing emotions can often be challenging. Engaging with your feelings requires practice and awareness. Here are several techniques designed to help you connect with and express your emotions more effectively.

1: Check-In with Your Body

Begin by finding a quiet and comfortable space where you can focus on yourself. Take a moment to close your eyes and take a few deep breaths. As you breathe in, notice how your body feels. Are there any areas of tension or discomfort? Pay attention to these physical sensations, as they often serve as signals for underlying emotions. Acknowledge where you hold stress or discomfort, allowing these feelings to guide your emotional awareness.

2: Label Your Emotions

Once you've checked in with your body, move on to identifying your emotions. Take a moment to reflect on what you are feeling. Are you experiencing anger, sadness, anxiety, or perhaps a mix of emotions? If you find it difficult to pinpoint your feelings, consider using an emotion wheel to assist you. This tool can help you label and articulate your emotions more clearly, providing a greater understanding of your emotional landscape.

3: Embrace Regular Practice and Use "I" Statements

Incorporate these techniques into your daily life to improve emotional regulation and communication. Regularly check in with your body and label your emotions to build awareness. Journaling a few times a week and using "I" statements in conversations—such as saying, "I feel angry when..." instead of "You make me angry"—can help you express emotions without blame, fostering healthier communication and reducing defensiveness. Consistent practice enhances your ability to manage emotions like anger effectively and encourages a greater sense of responsibility and empathy in relationships.

By utilizing these techniques for recognizing and expressing emotions, you empower yourself to engage with your feelings authentically. These practices foster emotional clarity and resilience, ultimately contributing to your overall well-being and mental health.

Exercise: 4-7-8 Breathing for Calming Anxiety

Exercise: 4-7-8 Breathing Technique: Cultivating Calm and Emotional Regulation

The 4-7-8 breathing technique is a simple yet powerful exercise that helps calm anxiety and activates the parasympathetic nervous system. This practice promotes relaxation and supports emotional regulation, making it an essential tool for managing stress.

1: Find a Comfortable Position

Begin by finding a comfortable seated position. You can sit in a chair with your feet flat on the ground or on the floor with your legs crossed. Ensure your back is straight and your shoulders are relaxed. You may close your eyes gently or softly focus on a point in front of you to minimize distractions.

2: Inhale for 4 Counts

Take a deep breath in through your nose for a count of four. As you inhale, feel your abdomen expand fully, allowing air to fill your lungs. Focus on the sensation of air entering your body, bringing with it a sense of calm and clarity.

3: Hold for 7 Counts

Once you have inhaled, hold your breath for a count of seven. During this pause, maintain a sense of calm and reassurance. Remind yourself that you are safe in this moment, and embrace the stillness within you.

4: Exhale for 8 Counts

Exhale slowly through your mouth for a count of eight. As you breathe out, visualize the release of tension or negative emotions. Feel your body relax as you let go of any stress or discomfort, creating space for peace and tranquility.

5: Repeat the Cycle

Complete this breathing cycle a total of four times. Inhale for four counts, hold for seven, and exhale for eight. With each cycle, notice a deeper sense of calm settling in your body and mind. Allow your breath to guide you into a state of relaxation.

6: Acknowledge Your Feelings

As you practice the 4-7-8 technique, be mindful of any emotions that arise. Are you feeling anxious, angry, or perhaps something else? Recognizing these emotions is essential, as it helps you understand and process your feelings more effectively.

7: Gradually Return to the Present

After completing four cycles of the breathing exercise, gently bring your awareness back to the present moment. Wiggle your fingers and toes, and take a few more deep breaths at your own pace. When you feel ready, slowly open your eyes and notice how your body and mind feel after this practice.

8: Practice Regularly

Incorporate the 4-7-8 breathing technique into your daily routine, especially during moments of anxiety or stress. Regular practice enhances your emotional regulation, making it easier to navigate challenging situations. With consistency, you will find yourself more resilient and better equipped to manage your emotions.

By integrating the 4-7-8 breathing technique into your self-care practices, you cultivate a greater sense of calm and emotional balance. This exercise empowers you to connect with your breath, fostering relaxation and enhancing your overall well-being.

Exercise: Aromatherapy for Relaxation and Emotional Resilience

Aromatherapy taps into the powerful connection between scent and memory, using essential oils to promote calmness and a sense of safety. As a somatic practice, it can enhance relaxation, emotional regulation, and overall well-being.

1. Choose Your Essential Oils

Select an essential oil based on your emotional needs. Lavender and chamomile are excellent for relaxation, while eucalyptus or peppermint can promote mental clarity. Choose scents that evoke positive associations or comforting memories, supporting a peaceful state of mind.

2. Create a Calming Environment

Begin by preparing a quiet, comfortable space. Diffuse the essential oil in the room, or place a few drops on a tissue or your wrist. Inhale deeply, allowing the scent to fill your senses. This intentional use of aroma helps you anchor into the present moment, creating a feeling of safety and grounding.

3. Practice Deep Breathing with the Aroma

As you inhale the scent, engage in slow, deep breathing. Breathe in through your nose, hold briefly, then exhale slowly through your mouth. This combination of scent and breath work can calm the nervous system, supporting emotional resilience and allowing you to process emotions more easily.

4. Reflect and Anchor Positive States

Notice any memories or positive emotions the aroma brings up, such as calm, warmth, or happiness. Allow these feelings to deepen, using the scent as a mental anchor. With regular practice, specific scents can become reminders of calmness and resilience, helping you maintain these states even in challenging situations.

Make Aromatherapy a Regular Practice

Integrating aromatherapy into your routine can foster relaxation and support emotional well-being, making it a valuable tool for self-care and stress management.

CHAPTER 7
TOUCH AND SELF-COMPASSION PRACTICES

Touch plays a vital role in self-soothing and cultivating self-compassion. It is a powerful way to connect with yourself, reduce self-criticism, and promote emotional healing. When you engage in touch-based practices, you activate the parasympathetic nervous system, which calms the body and mind. This helps you regulate your emotions, especially during stressful or overwhelming situations.

By incorporating touch into your self-care routine, you learn to show yourself kindness and support. Whether it's placing a hand on your heart or practicing self-massage, these small gestures create a sense of safety. They remind you that you deserve care and attention. Such practices help shift negative self-talk into more compassionate and supportive inner dialogue. Over time, engaging in these self-touch techniques can enhance emotional resilience and foster a deeper connection with your body.

Types of Practices

1. Self-Massage

Self-massage is a simple yet effective way to ease tension and promote relaxation. By applying gentle pressure to areas like your shoulders, neck, or feet, you can release muscle stiffness and activate calming sensations in the body. Self-massage not only helps reduce physical tension but also brings your awareness to your body, grounding you in the present moment. Using warm oil or lotion can enhance this experience, making it a nurturing and soothing practice.

2. Aromatherapy

Aromatherapy involves using essential oils to promote relaxation and emotional balance. Certain scents, like lavender or chamomile, have calming effects that can be paired with self-touch techniques. For instance, applying a few drops of essential oil to your wrists or temples and massaging them gently can help reduce stress and promote a sense of calm. Combining scent with touch deepens the soothing effect, as the fragrance stimulates the senses and enhances relaxation.

3. Acupressure

Acupressure is a traditional healing practice that involves applying pressure to specific points on the body. This practice can release tension, promote energy flow, and reduce stress. For example, pressing on points like the "Heart 7" (located on the wrist) can help calm anxiety. Acupressure allows you to connect with your body and relieve discomfort, encouraging a deeper sense of self-awareness and compassion.

4. Energy Healing

Energy healing practices, such as Reiki, focus on channeling energy to promote healing and balance in the body. You can use simple techniques like placing your hands over your heart, forehead, or belly to direct calming energy. This practice helps you connect with your body's natural energy flow, enhancing your sense of well-being. Even if you are not trained in formal energy healing, simply placing your hands on areas of tension or discomfort can provide a comforting and grounding sensation.

Exercise: Self-Soothing Touch

Self-soothing touch is a simple yet powerful practice you can use when feeling overwhelmed or anxious. By engaging in this exercise, you can foster a sense of calm and comfort, nurturing and supporting yourself through gentle touch.

1: Find a Quiet Space

Begin by finding a quiet space where you can sit or lie down comfortably without being disturbed. Ensure that you feel safe and at ease in this environment. Close your eyes and take a few deep breaths to center yourself, allowing your body to relax with each exhale.

2: Place a Hand on Your Chest

Gently place one or both hands on your chest, feeling the warmth radiating from your palms. Notice the rise and fall of your chest as you breathe, creating a soothing rhythm. This contact provides a deep sense of connection and safety, grounding you in the present moment.

3: Focus on the Sensation

Pay attention to the sensation of your hands on your chest. Allow the warmth and gentle pressure to create a sense of comfort. Visualize your hands transmitting care and compassion to yourself, enhancing your feeling of safety and nurturing.

4: Soothing Words

While you hold your hand in place, begin to say soothing phrases to yourself, such as "I'm here for you" or "It's okay to feel this way." Let these affirmations be a source of support and encouragement, allowing them to resonate within you and bring a sense of calm.

5: Notice Any Shifts

Remain in this position for a few minutes, observing any shifts in your body or emotions. You may notice your breath slowing down or your body relaxing more deeply. If you sense any tension, allow it to soften with each breath, embracing the warmth of your touch.

6: Release Slowly

When you feel ready, gently release your hands from your chest. Take a few deep breaths, allowing yourself to notice how you feel after this practice. Acknowledge any changes in your emotional state, reflecting on the comfort and support you have provided yourself.

7: Repeat When Needed

This practice can be repeated whenever you find yourself in need of a moment of comfort and grounding. Incorporating self-soothing touch into your routine helps cultivate a deeper connection to your body and emotions, promoting emotional resilience and well-being.

By engaging in self-soothing touch, you empower yourself to navigate moments of anxiety with greater ease. This technique encourages emotional awareness and provides a nurturing way to manage overwhelming feelings, ultimately fostering a sense of safety and comfort in your daily life..

Exercise: Massage Therapy Self-Care

Massage therapy is a calming and restorative practice that engages soft tissue manipulation to relieve muscle tension, reduce stress, and improve overall well-being. Though typically administered by trained therapists, you can integrate elements of massage into your self-care routine to promote relaxation and ease physical discomfort.

1. Find a Comfortable Space

Begin by choosing a quiet, comfortable place where you feel relaxed and at ease. Sit or lie down, close your eyes, and take several deep breaths to center yourself. This initial relaxation helps prepare your body for the soothing effects of self-massage.

2. Start with Gentle Shoulder and Neck Massage

Place your hands on your shoulders and gently knead the muscles, moving in small circles. Gradually work your way up to the neck, applying slight pressure to release tension. Focus on feeling the muscles soften under your touch, encouraging relaxation with each breath.

3. Apply Soothing Pressure to Your Hands and Feet

Use your thumbs to press and massage the center of your palms, then move to each finger, gently squeezing and releasing. For your feet, press down with your thumbs along the soles, focusing on any tight or sore areas. This practice can increase blood flow and bring relief to commonly overused areas.

Press your palms together - feel the pressure.

4. Tune Into the Sensations and Your Breath

As you massage, pay attention to the sensations under your touch and the rhythm of your breathing. This focus on sensation and breath activates the parasympathetic nervous system, reducing stress hormones like cortisol and promoting a calm state of mind.

5. End with a Calming Stretch

After massaging, stretch your arms overhead, roll your shoulders back, and take a few final deep breaths. Allow your body to fully relax, noticing any shifts in tension or mood. Conclude by acknowledging the comfort and relaxation you've provided yourself through this practice.

Incorporate Massage Therapy Regularly

By engaging in this self-massage routine, you create a consistent way to support relaxation and physical well-being. Regular practice enhances body awareness and fosters emotional resilience, helping you manage stress more effectively.

Exercise: Holistic Indian Head Massage for Stress Relief

Indian Head Massage is an Ayurvedic practice developed over 3,000 years ago in India. It targets marma points—areas of energy similar to acupressure points—to relieve stress, release toxins, and support relaxation. Focusing on the upper back, shoulders, neck, scalp, ears, and face, this massage can alleviate various physical and emotional strains, fostering mental clarity and overall well-being.

1. Begin with Shoulder and Upper Back Relaxation

Sit comfortably in a quiet space and start by gently massaging your shoulders and upper back. Using circular motions, apply pressure to ease muscular tension. This initial step prepares the body for deeper relaxation and promotes the release of built-up stress.

2. Massage the Neck and Scalp

Move up to the neck, applying gentle but firm pressure with your fingertips along both sides. Continue upward to the scalp, using your fingers to massage in slow circles. This technique can help improve lymphatic drainage and relieve headaches while stimulating mental clarity and concentration.

3. Focus on Marma Points Around the Face and Ears

Place your fingers near the temples, and with light pressure, massage in small circles, gradually moving down toward the jawline. For the ears, use gentle pinching and circular rubbing to stimulate these sensitive points, releasing negative emotions and promoting relaxation.

4. Incorporate Deep Breathing

Throughout the massage, focus on taking deep, steady breaths. Inhale deeply through your nose and exhale slowly through your mouth. This breathing technique enhances relaxation, helping to release sadness, grief, and other negative emotions, creating a sense of peace.

5. Finish with Gentle Strokes and Reflection

End the massage by gently stroking your forehead and temples, allowing your body and mind to settle. Take a moment to observe any changes in your mood, tension levels, or sense of calm. Regular practice can support mental concentration, promote hair health, and foster a sense of general well-being.

Practice Regularly for Long-Term Benefits

Incorporating Indian Head Massage into your routine can help alleviate stress, reduce muscle tension, and improve focus. This holistic approach fosters emotional and physical balance, supporting a journey toward deeper relaxation and resilience.

CHAPTER 8
ESTABLISHING ROUTINE AND STRUCTURE

Creating a daily routine that incorporates healthy habits and self-care practices is essential for maintaining mental and emotional well-being. In our fast-paced world, the importance of structure cannot be underestimated. A well-established routine provides a sense of stability and predictability, which can significantly reduce feelings of anxiety and overwhelm. By intentionally designing your day, you set the stage for nourishing your mind, body, and spirit, allowing you to function at your best.

A daily routine also fosters healthy habits, helping you prioritize activities that contribute to your overall well-being. When you create a schedule that includes self-care practices—such as exercise, healthy eating, mindfulness, and adequate rest—you are more likely to engage in these activities consistently. This consistency builds positive habits that can improve your mood, enhance your focus, and boost your resilience in the face of challenges.

In this chapter, we will explore two practical exercises designed to help you establish a daily routine that integrates healthy habits and self-care practices, setting the foundation for lasting well-being.

Exercise 1: Designing Your Ideal Daily Routine

Creating an ideal daily routine allows you to intentionally plan your day, incorporating healthy habits and self-care practices that support your well-being. This exercise guides you through the process of designing a personalized routine that reflects your needs and goals.

1: Reflect on Your Current Routine

Begin by reflecting on your current daily routine. Write down the activities you engage in, noting which ones contribute positively to your well-being and which ones may drain your energy. Identify any gaps where you could incorporate healthier habits or self-care practices.

2: Set Your Intentions

Consider what you want to achieve with your daily routine. What are your goals for physical health, mental clarity, and emotional well-being? Write down your intentions, focusing on specific areas you'd like to improve, such as increasing physical activity, practicing mindfulness, or fostering creativity.

3: Outline Your Ideal Day

Using a blank piece of paper or a digital tool, outline your ideal day. Start with the time you wake up and go through each hour, specifying what activities you'd like to include. Consider integrating healthy habits like morning exercise, balanced meals, work or study time, self-care breaks, and relaxation in the evening.

4: Prioritize Self-Care Practices

Within your outline, prioritize self-care practices. Identify times in your day where you can incorporate activities such as meditation, journaling, or engaging in hobbies. Be sure to allocate time for rest and relaxation to recharge your energy.

5: Incorporate Healthy Habits

As you finalize your routine, be mindful of including healthy habits that support your physical well-being. This can include regular meals, hydration, movement, and adequate sleep. Aim for a balanced approach that nourishes both your body and mind.

6: Create a Visual Representation

Once you have outlined your ideal routine, create a visual representation of it. This could be a colorful schedule or a chart that you can display in a prominent place, serving as a reminder of your intentions and goals. Visual cues can help reinforce your commitment to your new routine.

7: Implement and Adjust

Begin implementing your new routine gradually. Start by integrating a few elements at a time, allowing yourself to adjust as needed. Pay attention to how your routine affects your mood and energy levels, and feel free to make modifications based on what works best for you.

By designing your ideal daily routine, you empower yourself to prioritize healthy habits and self-care practices. This intentional approach fosters a sense of balance and stability in your life, enhancing your overall well-being.

Exercise 2: The Self-Care Schedule

The Self-Care Schedule is an exercise designed to help you intentionally carve out time for self-care within your daily routine. This practice encourages you to prioritize your well-being by scheduling specific activities that nurture your mind, body, and spirit.

1: Assess Your Current Schedule

Begin by assessing your current weekly schedule. Write down your commitments, responsibilities, and daily activities. Identify time slots where you can incorporate self-care practices, noting any gaps where you can create space for yourself.

2: Identify Self-Care Activities

Reflect on self-care activities that resonate with you. This may include activities such as reading, yoga, walking in nature, taking a relaxing bath, or practicing mindfulness. Write down a list of self-care practices you enjoy and want to incorporate into your routine.

3: Choose Specific Time Slots

Review your current schedule and select specific time slots for your self-care activities. Aim to dedicate at least a few minutes each day to self-care, whether it's in the morning, during lunch breaks, or in the evening. Choose times that work best for you and your lifestyle.

4: Create Your Self-Care Schedule

Using a calendar or planner, create a visual self-care schedule. Block off time for each self-care activity you've chosen, ensuring you allocate enough time to fully engage in each practice. Treat these time slots as non-negotiable appointments for your well-being.

5: Engage Fully in Self-Care

When the time for your self-care activity arrives, engage fully in the experience. Minimize distractions, put away your phone, and allow yourself to be present. Whether you are reading a book, practicing yoga, or enjoying a warm bath, savor each moment and the positive effects it brings.

By creating a Self-Care Schedule, you cultivate a deeper commitment to your well-being. This practice empowers you to prioritize your needs, fostering a healthier and more balanced life.

BOOK 4

Yoga

CHAPTER 1
THE FUNDAMENTALS OF YOGA

Yoga has ancient roots and has evolved over thousands of years, weaving together spiritual, philosophical, and physical traditions. Understanding yoga's history and philosophy is essential to highlight its relevance today, especially in relation to somatic therapy.

The Origins of Yoga

Yoga's origins trace back over 5,000 years to the Indus Valley civilization, now part of India and Pakistan. The Rigveda, one of the earliest sacred texts, dates back to around 1500 BCE and describes yoga in the context of rituals and meditation aimed at spiritual enlightenment. As time passed, yoga incorporated philosophy, ethics, and metaphysics, shaping the diverse forms we see today.

The term "yoga" comes from the Sanskrit word "yuj," which means "to unite" or "to join." This unification refers to the connection between body, mind, and spirit, as well as the integration of individual consciousness with universal consciousness. This foundational principle remains crucial in your yoga practice.

Classical Yoga and the Yoga Sutras

The Yoga Sutras of Patanjali are the most influential text on yoga, composed around the 2nd century BCE. Patanjali's work compiles aphorisms outlining yoga's philosophy and practice, introducing the eight limbs of yoga, known as Ashtanga Yoga. These limbs guide your personal development and spiritual growth:

1. Yama (Ethical Disciplines): Moral codes governing interactions with others, such as non-violence (ahimsa) and truthfulness (satya).
2. Niyama (Personal Observances): Guidelines for self-discipline, including cleanliness (saucha) and contentment (santosha).
3. Asana (Postures): Physical postures that prepare your body for meditation and promote health.
4. Pranayama (Breath Control): Techniques regulating your breath, enhancing prana (life force), and cultivating awareness.
5. Pratyahara (Withdrawal of the Senses): The practice of turning inward and disengaging from distractions.

6. Dharana (Concentration): Focusing your mind on a single point or object to cultivate mental clarity.

7. Dhyana (Meditation): A deeper awareness where your mind absorbs the object of meditation.

8. Samadhi (Union or Bliss): The ultimate state of consciousness where the individual self merges with the universal self.

These eight limbs provide a framework for your yoga practice, guiding you toward self-realization and enlightenment. Patanjali's teachings emphasize that yoga is not just physical; it integrates ethical, mental, and spiritual dimensions.

The Philosophical Underpinnings

Yoga's philosophical foundations are rooted in Indian philosophical systems, including Samkhya, Vedanta, and Buddhism. Samkhya philosophy presents a dualistic worldview that distinguishes between Purusha (consciousness) and Prakriti (matter). This perspective highlights yoga's aim to transcend the mind's fluctuations in search of liberation (moksha).

Vedanta focuses on reality and the self, teaching that the true self (Atman) is eternal and identical to universal consciousness (Brahman). Realizing this truth is central to your yoga practice, encouraging you to move beyond ego identification and discover your inherent divinity.

Buddhism contributes to yoga's evolution, especially in mindfulness and meditation. The Buddhist practice of Vipassana (insight meditation) shares similarities with yoga's meditative aspects. Both emphasize awareness, presence, and understanding the nature of suffering.

As yoga spread beyond India, it integrated with various cultures, leading to diverse styles and practices. The 19th and 20th centuries marked a turning point for yoga as it gained popularity in the West. Pioneers like Swami Vivekananda and Krishnamacharya introduced yoga to Western audiences, emphasizing its physical and mental health benefits.

Today, yoga encompasses many styles, including Hatha, Vinyasa, Ashtanga, Iyengar, Kundalini, and Restorative. Each style has its unique approach and emphasis. Despite these variations, the core principles of yoga remain constant: self-awareness, compassion, and connection.

Different Styles of Yoga

Yoga offers diverse styles and practices, catering to various preferences and goals. Each style emphasizes different aspects of practice, making yoga accessible and adaptable to support your physical, mental, and spiritual well-being. Here's a look at popular yoga styles and their unique characteristics.

1. Hatha Yoga

Hatha Yoga introduces foundational poses and breathwork, serving as a starting point for many other yoga styles. Classes emphasize alignment and gentle stretching.

Benefits:

- Improves flexibility and strength.

- Promotes relaxation and stress relief.

- Enhances awareness of your body and breath.

2. Vinyasa Yoga

Known for its fluid, dance-like transitions, Vinyasa Yoga synchronizes movement with breath, creating a dynamic and often creative practice.

Benefits:

- Increases cardiovascular fitness and endurance.

- Enhances strength and flexibility.

- Encourages mindfulness through breath and movement synchronization.

3. Ashtanga Yoga

A structured and physically demanding practice, Ashtanga follows a specific sequence of poses that develop strength, flexibility, and stamina.

Benefits:

- Builds physical strength and endurance.

- Enhances mental focus and discipline.

- Supports detoxification through continuous movement and breath.

4. Iyengar Yoga

Iyengar Yoga focuses on precise alignment, often using props to support each pose. This makes it accessible and safe for people of all levels, especially beginners or those recovering from injuries.

Benefits:

- Improves postural alignment and body awareness.

- Increases strength and flexibility.

- Facilitates rehabilitation from injuries.

5. Kundalini Yoga

This style combines postures, breathwork, chanting, and meditation with the aim of awakening energy along the spine, often bringing about a transformative experience.

Benefits:

- Enhances spiritual awareness and personal growth.

- Increases energy levels and vitality.

- Reduces stress and anxiety through breath and meditation.

6. Restorative Yoga

With a focus on deep relaxation, Restorative Yoga uses props and passive stretches, allowing your body and mind to release tension and find rest.

Benefits:

- Reduces stress and promotes relaxation.

- Aids recovery from injury or illness.

- Encourages mindfulness and introspection.

7. Yin Yoga

Yin Yoga involves long-held stretches that target connective tissues, fostering calmness and flexibility in a tranquil setting.

Benefits:

- Increases flexibility and joint mobility.

- Promotes mental calmness and focus.

- Supports emotional release and self-awareness.

8. Power Yoga

An energetic and adaptable style, Power Yoga is inspired by Ashtanga but emphasizes strength, stamina, and challenging postures.

Benefits:

- Builds muscle strength and endurance.

- Improves cardiovascular fitness.

- Enhances mental focus and concentration.

9. Bikram Yoga

Practiced in a heated room, Bikram Yoga consists of a set sequence of 26 poses, encouraging flexibility, sweating, and focus.

Benefits:

- Enhances flexibility and cardiovascular fitness.

- Promotes detoxification through sweating.

- Improves mental clarity and focus.

10. Sivananda Yoga

Sivananda Yoga takes a holistic approach, integrating postures, breathing, relaxation, and meditation for comprehensive well-being.

Benefits:

- Promotes overall health and well-being.

- Encourages a balanced lifestyle.

- Enhances mental clarity and emotional stability.

Yoga offers diverse paths to holistic wellness. Experimenting with different styles can deepen self-understanding and help you find the right practice for your unique needs and goals.

CHAPTER 2
THE SYNERGY OF YOGA AND SOMATIC THERAPY

Integrating yoga and somatic therapy offers a powerful healing approach, emphasizing the interconnectedness of body and mind. Both practices promote awareness of bodily sensations and emotions, providing tools for self-discovery and emotional regulation. This chapter explores how yoga enhances somatic therapy and highlights the shared principles that support personal transformation.

Yoga and somatic therapy share core principles. Both emphasize the body's role in emotional healing. They recognize that emotions manifest physically. These practices encourage you to connect with your body, fostering self-awareness and understanding.

Key commonalities include:

1. Mind-Body Connection: Both approaches highlight the importance of being present in your body. They facilitate awareness of physical sensations and emotional states.

2. Breath Awareness: Breath is central to both practices. It regulates energy and promotes relaxation. Conscious breathing enhances emotional processing.

3. Movement and Expression: Movement is vital for releasing tension and expressing emotions. Yoga offers various postures and flows that encourage physical release. Somatic therapy includes movement techniques to process trauma and stress.

4. Presence and Mindfulness: Practicing mindfulness is crucial in both approaches. Mindfulness cultivates acceptance of present experiences without judgment.

The Benefits of Integration

Integrating yoga with somatic therapy enhances healing. This synergy offers unique benefits:

- Enhanced Body Awareness: Combining yoga postures with somatic exercises fosters greater awareness of bodily sensations. This heightened awareness helps you recognize emotional patterns stored in your body.
- Release of Trauma: Both practices provide tools for releasing stored

trauma. Yoga postures create space for physical release, while somatic therapy techniques guide you through emotional processing.

- Emotional Regulation: Practicing yoga cultivates emotional resilience. The breath control and mindfulness techniques from yoga help you manage stress and anxiety.
- Increased Relaxation: The integration of gentle yoga and somatic techniques promotes deep relaxation, allowing you to access your inner experiences more readily.

Practical Applications

Incorporating yoga into somatic therapy sessions can be transformative. Here are practical applications:

1. **Warm-Up Movements:** Begin sessions with gentle yoga movements to prepare your body. This practice can increase awareness and readiness for deeper somatic work.

2. **Breathwork Integration:** Use breathwork techniques from yoga to regulate your emotions. Focus on your breath during somatic exercises.

3. **Mindful Movement:** Integrate yoga postures that align with somatic exercises. For example, use cat-cow stretches to explore spinal movement and release tension.

4. **Meditative Practices:** Conclude sessions with meditation or guided relaxation. This practice helps you integrate the experiences and insights gained during the session.

Integrating yoga with somatic therapy creates a holistic approach to healing. This integration emphasizes the importance of body awareness and emotional processing. By combining these practices, you can experience profound transformation, cultivating resilience, self-awareness, and emotional regulation. Exploring this synergy enhances your journey toward healing and self-discovery.

CHAPTER 3
STRESS RELIEF THROUGH YOGA

Yoga offers a powerful way to relieve stress. In the context of somatic therapy, it helps you connect with your body. This connection is essential for processing stress and emotions. Here's how yoga can be beneficial for stress relief through somatic therapy.

First, yoga encourages you to become aware of your body. You learn to notice where you hold tension. For example, you might feel tightness in your shoulders or jaw. By recognizing these sensations, you can start to release them. This awareness is a key aspect of somatic therapy. It allows you to understand how your body reacts to stress.

In yoga, you practice various postures (asanas) that promote relaxation. Poses like Child's Pose and Corpse Pose help you let go of tension. They allow you to sink into a state of calm. As you hold these poses, you can focus on your breath. Deep, mindful breathing helps reduce anxiety and stress. It calms your nervous system and brings you back to the present moment.

Somatic therapy emphasizes the importance of breathing. In yoga, you learn breath control through techniques like Pranayama. These practices teach you to use your breath as a tool for relaxation. When you feel stress creeping in, you can use your breath to regain control. This skill can be empowering and help you manage stress in daily life.

Additionally, yoga encourages grounding. Grounding techniques in yoga connect you to the earth. They provide a sense of stability and safety. When you feel grounded, you are less likely to feel overwhelmed by stress. This grounding helps you develop resilience and cope better with challenges.

Another benefit of yoga is emotional release. During your practice, you may experience emotions that arise. This can happen in certain poses, especially hip openers. In somatic therapy, you learn to embrace these emotions without judgment. Yoga creates a safe space for you to process and release these feelings.

Shavasana (Corpse Pose)

Shavasana, commonly known as Corpse Pose, is a restorative posture practiced at the end of a yoga session. This pose promotes deep relaxation and helps to calm the nervous system. Despite its simplicity, Shavasana is a powerful tool for reducing stress and anxiety.

Shavasana offers numerous benefits, particularly in relation to stress relief. By allowing your body to rest completely, you give yourself a chance to recharge physically and mentally. This pose calms the mind and nervous system, reducing the effects of stress and anxiety.

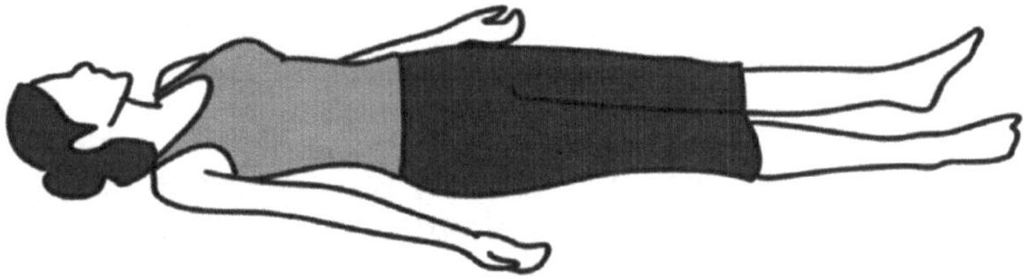

As you breathe deeply, you signal your body to enter a state of relaxation. This practice slows the heart rate, lowers blood pressure, and decreases muscle tension. The stillness of Shavasana creates space for introspection, helping you process emotions and thoughts without distractions.

1. To enter Shavasana a, lie flat on your back on a comfortable surface, such as a yoga mat

2. Allow your feet to fall naturally to the sides, ensuring your body is straight and aligned

3. Place your arms alongside your body with palms facing up, promoting openness

4. Close your eyes and take deep, slow breaths

5. Focus on relaxing each part of your body, from your toes to your head.

Balasana (Child's Pose)

Balasana, or Child's Pose, is a gentle and restorative posture that encourages introspection and relaxation. This pose mimics a fetal position, providing a sense of safety and comfort. Balasana is often used as a resting pose throughout a yoga practice, allowing you to reconnect with your breath and body.

Balasana offers a wide range of benefits, particularly in relation to stress relief and emotional well-being. This pose encourages the release of tension in the back, shoulders, and neck. By folding forward, you create a gentle compression in the abdomen, stimulating digestion and promoting relaxation.

The calming nature of Balasana helps to reduce anxiety and stress. As you settle into the pose, your breath slows, allowing your mind to quiet down. This introspective quality of Balasana makes it an excellent tool for self-reflection and emotional processing.

How to Practice Balasana:

1. To enter Balasana, start by kneeling on the mat with your big toes touching and knees spread apart

2. Sit back on your heels, then slowly fold forward, resting your forehead on the mat

3. Extend your arms alongside your body with palms facing up or stretch them forward to deepen the stretch

4. Close your eyes and take slow, deep breaths, allowing your body to relax into the pose.

Viparita Karani (Legs-Up-the-Wall Pose)

Viparita Karani, or Legs-Up-the-Wall Pose, is a restorative posture that calms the mind and promotes relaxation. This pose is often recommended for its ability to reduce anxiety and improve blood circulation. By elevating your legs, you create a gentle inversion that offers numerous benefits for both the body and mind.

How to Practice Viparita Karani:

1. To enter Viparita Karani, find a wall and sit with one hip against it

2. Swing your legs up the wall while lowering your back to the floor

3. Your body should form an L-shape, with your legs resting vertically and your back flat on the ground

4. If needed, place a folded blanket or bolster under your hips for added support

5. Allow your arms to rest alongside your body or place them on your abdomen

6. Close your eyes and breathe deeply, letting go of any tension in your body.

CHAPTER 4
MANAGING ANXIETY WITH YOGA

Yoga is a powerful tool for reducing anxiety. It combines movement, breath, and mindfulness. This holistic approach helps you connect with your body. When you practice yoga, you become more aware of your physical sensations. This awareness can create a sense of safety and grounding.

The physical postures in yoga release tension. As you stretch and strengthen your body, you let go of stress. Each pose encourages you to breathe deeply. Deep breathing activates your parasympathetic nervous system. This response calms your body and mind. It lowers your heart rate and reduces feelings of anxiety.

Mindfulness is a key element in yoga. It teaches you to stay present. When you focus on your breath or movement, your mind quiets. You learn to observe your thoughts without judgment. This practice helps you detach from anxious thoughts. You realize that thoughts are not facts. You can let them go more easily.

Yoga also promotes relaxation. Poses like Avasana (Corpse Pose) and Balasana (Child's Pose) encourage deep rest. These restorative poses calm your nervous system. They provide space for introspection. In these moments, you can process your feelings and emotions.

In somatic therapy, the body is viewed as a source of wisdom. Yoga honors this connection. It helps you listen to your body's needs. By tuning into your physical sensations, you can identify where you hold tension or anxiety. This awareness can facilitate emotional release.

Incorporating yoga into your routine can significantly reduce anxiety. It offers you practical tools for managing stress. With consistent practice, you can cultivate a sense of calm and balance in your life. You empower yourself to navigate challenges with greater resilience.

Marjaryasana-Bitilasana (Cat-Cow Stretch)

Marjaryasana-Bitilasana provides numerous benefits for both body and mind. This gentle flow releases tension in your back and neck, promoting relaxation. It also enhances spinal flexibility, which can alleviate discomfort caused by prolonged sitting. As you move through Cat-Cow, you cultivate mindfulness and body awareness, tuning into how your body feels during each transition.

This practice can also serve as a moving meditation, allowing you to connect with your emotions and thoughts in a safe space. The rhythmic movement encourages deep breathing, which enhances relaxation and reduces stress levels. By regularly practicing Marjaryasana-Bitilasana, you create a greater sense of balance in your life, making it easier to cope with anxiety. The gentle flow helps release emotional blockages, allowing for a clearer mind and a more centered state.

How to Practice Marjaryasana-Bitilasana:

1. To practice Marjaryasana-Bitilasana, begin on your hands and knees in a tabletop position

2. Ensure your wrists are aligned under your shoulders and your knees are directly beneath your hips

3. Inhale deeply and arch your back, lifting your head and tailbone toward the ceiling (Cat Pose)

4. Allow your belly to soften toward the mat

5. As you exhale, round your spine, tucking your chin to your chest and pulling your belly button in (Cow Pose)

6. Continue to flow between these two movements, coordinating your breath with your motions

7. Inhale as you enter Cow Pose, and exhale as you transition into Cat Pose

8. Repeat this sequence for several rounds, focusing on the sensations in your spine and body.

Upward-Facing Dog Pose (Ūrdhva Mukha Svānāsana)

Upward-Facing Dog is an energizing pose that offers numerous benefits. This backbend opens the chest and strengthens the spine, which can uplift your mood and promote a sense of vitality. By encouraging deeper breathing, this pose enhances your overall well-being and helps to combat fatigue. The heart-opening aspect of Upward-Facing Dog fosters feelings of positivity, helping to counteract stress and anxiety.

As you lift your chest and heart, you embrace vulnerability and resilience. This pose can also improve your posture, allowing you to feel more confident and grounded. Over time, regular practice of Upward-Facing Dog can help you develop greater strength and flexibility in your back, enhancing your overall physical health.

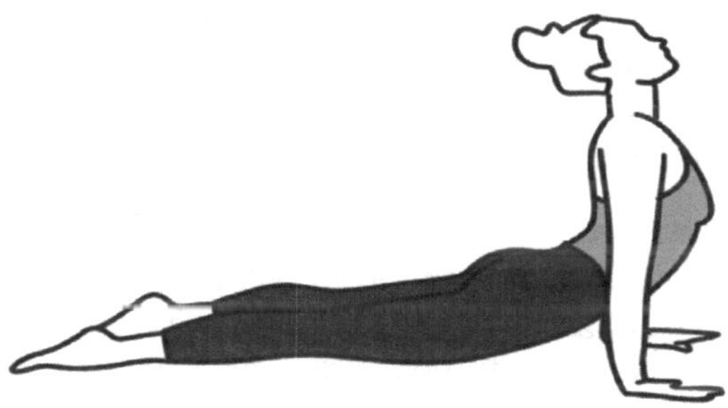

How to Practice Upward-Facing Dog Pose:

1. To enter Upward-Facing Dog, start by lying flat on your stomach with your legs extended behind you

2. Place your hands under your shoulders, fingers spread wide, and keep your elbows close to your body

3. Inhale deeply as you press into your palms, lifting your chest and thighs off the ground

4. Straighten your arms and open your heart toward the ceiling, relaxing your shoulders away from your ears

5. Keep your gaze slightly upward, but avoid straining your neck

6. Hold the pose for several breaths, focusing on the expansion in your chest and the strength in your back

7. To release, exhale as you lower your body back down to the mat.

CHAPTER 5
THE POWER OF MEDITATION

Yoga serves as a powerful tool for meditation and mindfulness. It helps you connect with your body and mind, fostering a deeper awareness of the present moment. Through yoga, you learn to quiet your thoughts and focus on your breath. This practice creates space for mindfulness, allowing you to observe your emotions without judgment.

Incorporating yoga into your daily routine enhances your ability to meditate. Each pose encourages you to be present. You can tune into your body's sensations and feelings. This heightened awareness brings clarity to your thoughts. As you flow through poses, you develop a greater understanding of how your body holds stress and tension.

Mindfulness in yoga is about being fully engaged in each movement. You learn to breathe deeply and rhythmically, grounding yourself in the here and now. This mindful approach to movement helps you release distractions. You can let go of worries about the past or future. Instead, you focus on your breath and body. This practice cultivates a sense of calm and peace.

Yoga also incorporates various meditation techniques. You can practice breath awareness, visualization, or loving-kindness meditation. These techniques enhance your mindfulness practice. They help you cultivate compassion for yourself and others. You learn to observe your thoughts without getting caught up in them. This non-judgmental awareness can lead to emotional healing.

Additionally, yoga teaches you to listen to your body. You become more attuned to your physical sensations, emotions, and thoughts. This connection helps you recognize patterns of stress or anxiety. You learn to respond to these sensations with kindness. This compassionate awareness fosters a sense of safety within yourself.

The combination of movement, breath, and meditation in yoga creates a holistic practice. It allows you to explore your inner landscape. You can gain insights into your mental and emotional well-being. Over time, you may find that your ability to meditate improves. You become more focused and centered, even outside of your yoga practice.

Pranayama (Breath Control)

Pranayama, particularly Nadi Shodhana, offers profound benefits for mindfulness and mental clarity. This technique helps balance the nervous system, reducing feelings of anxiety and stress. By consciously controlling your breath, you create a sense of calm and focus. Pranayama encourages you to tune into your body, enhancing your awareness of physical sensations and emotional states. This heightened mindfulness fosters a greater understanding of your thought patterns and feelings.

Regular practice of Pranayama can improve lung capacity and enhance oxygen flow in your body. This promotes overall physical health and vitality. As you practice, you may find that your mind becomes clearer and more centered. The rhythmic nature of breath control encourages a meditative state, helping to quiet racing thoughts and promote relaxation. Over time, incorporating Pranayama into your routine can lead to a deeper sense of peace and well-being.

How to Practice Pranayama:

1. Find a quiet space and sit comfortably on the floor or in a chair.

2. Close your eyes gently and take a moment to notice your natural breath.

3. Begin with Nadi Shodhana (Alternate Nostril Breathing):

- Use your right thumb to close your right nostril.

- Inhale deeply through your left nostril for a count of four.

4. Close your left nostril with your ring finger and release your thumb from the right nostril.

5. Exhale through the right nostril for a count of four.

6. Inhale through the right nostril, close it, and exhale through the left nostril.

7. Continue this alternating pattern for several rounds, focusing on your breath.

8. Keep your posture straight and relaxed, allowing the breath to flow naturally.

Padmasana (Lotus Pose)

Padmasana is a classic seated pose that offers numerous benefits, particularly for meditation. This pose promotes physical stability and mental calmness. By grounding your body, you create a solid base for deep introspection and focus. The crossed legs help to open the hips and stretch the knees, enhancing flexibility over time.

In Padmasana, your upright posture encourages proper alignment of the spine, facilitating optimal breath flow. This alignment supports effective meditation practice, allowing you to remain alert yet relaxed. As you settle into the pose, you may find that your mind quiets, making space for deeper meditation.

Moreover, Padmasana encourages a sense of balance and harmony in both body and mind. This pose can help alleviate stress and anxiety, promoting emotional stability. Regular practice of Padmasana can enhance your ability to sit for extended periods, deepening your meditation practice.

How to Practice Padmasana:

1. Begin by sitting on the floor with your legs extended in front of you.

2. Bend your right knee and bring your right foot to rest on your left thigh, with the sole facing upward.

3. Bend your left knee and place your left foot on your right thigh.

4. Ensure that your feet are positioned so that the soles are facing upward.

5. Sit up tall, aligning your spine and shoulders over your hips.

6. Rest your hands on your knees, palms facing up or down.

7. Close your eyes and take several deep breaths, allowing your body to relax into the pose.

Ardha Padmasana (Half Lotus Pose)

Ardha Padmasana serves as a gentle alternative to Padmasana, making it accessible for many practitioners. This pose offers several benefits, especially in promoting relaxation and mindfulness. By engaging in this seated position, you create a stable base for meditation. It helps to calm the mind and encourages focus on the present moment.

How to Practice Ardha Padmasana:

1. Begin by sitting comfortably on the floor with your legs extended in front of you.

2. Bend your right knee and bring your right foot to rest on your left thigh, with the sole facing upward.

3. Keep your left leg extended on the floor.

4. Sit up tall, ensuring your spine is straight and your shoulders are relaxed.

5. Rest your hands on your knees, palms facing up or down.

6. Close your eyes and take deep, steady breaths.

7. Focus on your breath and the sensations in your body, allowing yourself to relax into the pose.

CHAPTER 6
ENERGIZING YOUR BODY

Yoga serves as a powerful form of somatic therapy that can significantly boost energy levels and build physical strength. By engaging both the body and mind, yoga promotes a holistic approach to enhancing your overall vitality.

When you practice yoga, you focus on mindful movement and breath awareness. This connection between breath and movement stimulates the body's energy pathways. As you flow through poses, you cultivate a sense of vitality and presence. This heightened awareness allows you to tap into your inner resources, reducing feelings of fatigue and lethargy.

Certain yoga poses are particularly effective for boosting energy. For example, standing poses engage the legs, core, and arms, promoting strength and stability. As you hold these poses, your muscles work to maintain balance, enhancing overall physical strength. This physical engagement helps increase blood flow and oxygenation throughout the body, contributing to a sense of revitalization.

In addition to physical strength, yoga fosters mental resilience. The combination of movement, breath, and meditation encourages a positive mindset. As you navigate challenges on the mat, you develop a greater sense of determination and perseverance. This mental strength translates to daily life, empowering you to face obstacles with confidence.

The breath plays a crucial role in energy enhancement during yoga practice. These techniques invigorate the body while promoting calmness. By focusing on your breath, you can harness energy from within and distribute it throughout your body. This practice not only increases your energy but also helps you manage stress, allowing for a more balanced emotional state.

Furthermore, yoga encourages a deeper connection with your body. As you engage in various poses, you become more attuned to physical sensations and limitations. This awareness fosters a sense of empowerment, motivating you to push your boundaries and cultivate strength over time.

Tadasana (Mountain Pose)

Tadasana, or Mountain Pose, serves as a foundational posture in yoga that offers a range of benefits. This pose promotes stability and energy while grounding you in the present moment. By practicing Tadasana, you cultivate a sense of balance, both physically and mentally.

Standing tall helps to improve posture and alignment. As you engage your core and leg muscles, you strengthen the foundation of your body. This alignment encourages better body mechanics in daily life, reducing the risk of injury.

Tadasana also promotes mindfulness. By focusing on your breath and maintaining stillness, you enhance your ability to stay present. This awareness can help you cultivate a more centered state of mind, allowing you to manage stress and anxiety more effectively.

How to Practice Tadasana (Mountain Pose):

1. Stand tall with your feet together or hip-width apart, grounding your weight evenly on both feet.

2. Distribute your weight equally between your heels and the balls of your feet.

3. Engage your leg muscles, lifting your kneecaps slightly to activate your thighs.

4. Lengthen your spine by reaching the crown of your head toward the ceiling.

5. Relax your shoulders away from your ears and keep your arms by your sides, palms facing your body.

6. Take a deep breath in, feeling your chest expand, and lift your arms overhead if comfortable.

7. Keep your gaze forward, focusing on a point in front of you to maintain balance.

8. Hold the pose for 30 seconds to 1 minute, breathing deeply and steadily throughout.

Trikonasana (Triangle Pose)

Trikonasana, or Triangle Pose, is a powerful posture that offers numerous benefits for the body and mind. This pose strengthens the legs and opens the chest, invigorating your entire system.

The stretching and strengthening of the legs enhance overall stability and support balance. As you extend your body from side to side, you create a deep stretch in your hamstrings and inner thighs, promoting flexibility. This lengthening also helps to relieve tension in the lower back.

Additionally, Trikonasana cultivates mental clarity. The alignment and engagement required in this pose encourage mindfulness, allowing you to stay present and focused. By concentrating on your breath and maintaining balance, you can reduce feelings of stress and anxiety.

Practicing Triangle Pose can also foster a sense of empowerment and confidence. As you hold the pose, you engage your core and leg muscles, which can enhance your physical strength. This physical strength translates into mental resilience, encouraging you to embrace challenges in your daily life.

How to Practice Trikonasana (Triangle Pose):

1. Begin by standing with your feet wide apart, about 3 to 4 feet.

2. Turn your right foot out 90 degrees and your left foot slightly in.

3. Extend your arms parallel to the floor, reaching them out to the sides.

4. Inhale deeply, and as you exhale, hinge at your hip to lower your right hand toward your right ankle.

5. Keep your left arm reaching toward the ceiling, creating a straight line

from your left fingertips to your left heel.

6. Turn your head to gaze up at your left hand, if comfortable, or look straight ahead.

7. Ensure both legs remain straight and strong, grounding through your feet.

8. Hold the pose for 30 seconds to 1 minute, breathing deeply, then switch sides.

Navasana (Boat Pose)

Navasana, or Boat Pose, is a dynamic posture that offers numerous benefits, particularly for your core and overall energy levels. This pose strengthens the core muscles, enhancing stability and balance.

Boat Pose boosts energy levels by stimulating the digestive system. As you hold this pose, you compress and engage your abdominal organs, promoting circulation and digestion. This activation can help combat fatigue, enhancing your overall vitality.

Additionally, Navasana fosters mental focus and concentration. Balancing on your sit bones requires coordination and awareness. This practice of staying present can help you develop greater mindfulness, reducing feelings of stress and anxiety.

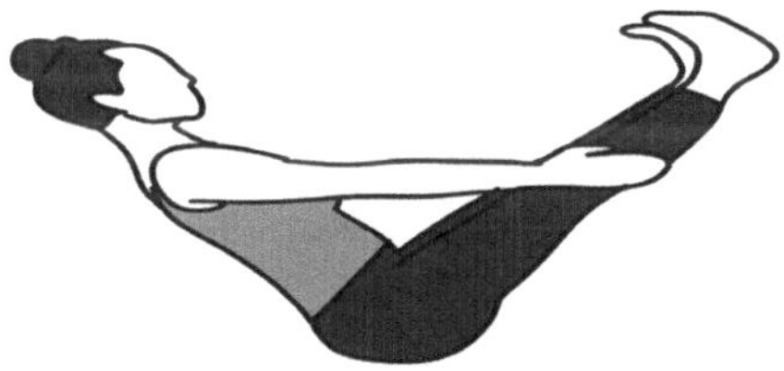

How to Practice Navasana (Boat Pose):

1. Begin by sitting on the floor with your knees bent and feet flat on the mat.

2. Lean back slightly, keeping your spine straight, and lift your feet off the floor.

3. Bring your shins parallel to the ground, or extend your legs straight if comfortable.

4. Reach your arms forward, parallel to the floor, with palms facing each other.

5. Engage your core muscles to maintain balance and stability.

6. Keep your chest lifted and shoulders relaxed, avoiding tension in your neck.

7. Hold the pose for 15 to 30 seconds, breathing deeply, then lower your feet back to the mat to release.

CHAPTER 7
YOGA FOR OVERCOMING DEPRESSION

Yoga can be a powerful tool in managing depression. It encourages you to reconnect with your body and emotions. This connection is crucial for understanding your feelings and fostering healing.

Through yoga, you can explore different postures and movements. These physical activities help release pent-up tension. As you move, you may notice areas of tightness or discomfort. Acknowledging these sensations can promote emotional awareness. This process allows you to better understand what you are experiencing internally.

Breath is an essential part of yoga. Focusing on your breath can calm your mind. Deep breathing techniques help you slow down. They create a sense of space and ease in your body. This practice also reduces the effects of stress and anxiety. By calming your nervous system, you create an environment conducive to healing.

In yoga, you can incorporate mindfulness. Mindfulness involves paying attention to the present moment. As you practice, you can observe your thoughts and feelings without judgment. This non-reactive awareness can help you process emotions more effectively. It allows you to move away from negative thought patterns. You can learn to respond to your feelings instead of reacting impulsively.

Physical movement in yoga releases endorphins, which are natural mood lifters. The gentle stretching and strengthening of muscles can lead to improved energy levels. Over time, consistent practice can help you feel more balanced and stable. You may notice a decrease in feelings of sadness or hopelessness.

Yoga also encourages self-compassion. As you practice, you learn to be kinder to yourself. You may find that you can let go of self-criticism. This shift in mindset can be transformative. It creates a more nurturing internal dialogue.

Incorporating restorative poses into your routine can be especially beneficial as they promote relaxation, allowing you to rest and recharge.

In conclusion, yoga as somatic therapy can be an effective approach to managing depression. By fostering a connection between body and mind, you create space for healing and self-discovery.

Bound Angle Pose (Supta Baddha Konasana)

Reclining Bound Angle Pose (Supta Baddha Konasana) is a deeply relaxing posture with numerous benefits for both body and mind. This pose encourages a sense of openness and vulnerability, inviting you to let go of tension and stress.

Additionally, Supta Baddha Konasana calms the nervous system, making it an excellent pose for stress relief. By focusing on your breath, you activate the relaxation response in your body, lowering heart rate and blood pressure. This calming effect can help alleviate feelings of anxiety or overwhelm, fostering emotional balance.

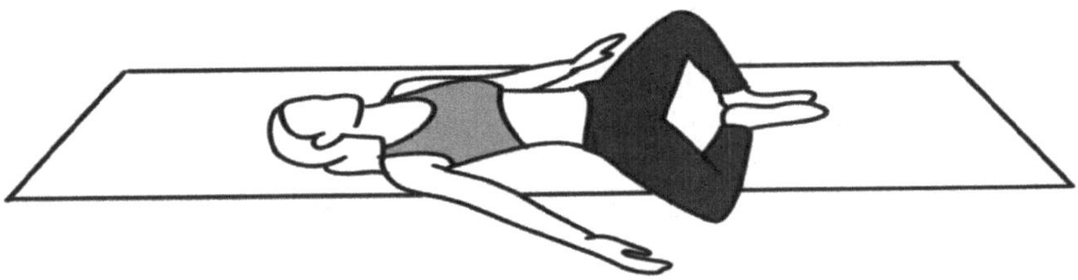

How to Practice Reclining Bound Angle Pose (Supta Baddha Konasana):

1. Begin by lying flat on your back on a comfortable surface, like a yoga mat.

2. Bring the soles of your feet together, allowing your knees to fall open to the sides.

3. Adjust your position so that your feet are a few inches away from your pelvis, creating a gentle stretch in your inner thighs.

4. Rest your arms alongside your body, palms facing up, which promotes openness and relaxation.

5. Close your eyes and take slow, deep breaths, focusing on the sensations in your body.

6. If comfortable, place a cushion or block under each knee for additional support.

7. Allow your back to relax into the mat and let go of any tension in your body.

8. Stay in this position for 5 to 15 minutes, allowing yourself to fully relax and surrender to gravity.

Shiitali Kumbhaka (Cooling Breath)

Shiitali Kumbhaka, or Cooling Breath, is an excellent pranayama technique for regulating body temperature and calming the mind. This practice is especially beneficial in hot weather or during periods of high stress. The cool air entering your body soothes both physically and emotionally.

This technique promotes a sense of relaxation and tranquility. The cooling effect can help alleviate feelings of anger or frustration. By calming the mind, Shiitali Kumbhaka allows for clearer thinking and improved concentration.

Regular practice of this breathing technique can help reduce anxiety and promote emotional balance. The cooling quality of Shiitali Kumbhaka invites a sense of peace and stillness, allowing you to reconnect with your inner self.

How to Practice Shiitali Kumbhaka:

1. Sit comfortably in a cross-legged position with your spine straight.

2. Stick your tongue out and curl the sides to form a tube, creating a straw-like shape.

3. Inhale deeply through your curled tongue, feeling the cool air entering your mouth.

4. Close your mouth and hold your breath for a moment.

5. Exhale slowly through your nose, allowing your body to relax.

6. Repeat this process for several rounds, focusing on the cooling sensation and calming effects.

CHAPTER 8
MASTERING BREATH AWARENESS AND CONTROL

Yoga offers profound benefits in somatic therapy, particularly through the practice of breathwork. Breath is not only essential for life; it is also a powerful tool for emotional regulation, physical well-being, and mindfulness. By integrating breath awareness into yoga, you can tap into the body's innate ability to heal and restore balance.

One of the primary benefits of yoga breathing techniques, or pranayama, is their ability to reduce stress and anxiety. When you focus on your breath, you engage the parasympathetic nervous system, which activates the body's relaxation response. This helps to lower heart rate, decrease blood pressure, and reduce muscle tension. As you inhale deeply and exhale slowly, you create a sense of calmness that can ease feelings of overwhelm.

Moreover, conscious breathing can enhance your emotional awareness. In somatic therapy, understanding your emotions is crucial for healing. As you practice different breathing techniques, such as Ujjayi or Nadi Shodhana, you become more attuned to your body's sensations and emotional states. This heightened awareness allows you to identify areas of tension or discomfort, facilitating a process of emotional release and healing.

Breathwork in yoga also fosters mindfulness. By concentrating on your breath, you anchor yourself in the present moment. This practice can counteract negative thought patterns and help you break free from rumination. Mindfulness through breath encourages you to observe your thoughts and feelings without judgment. This non-reactive awareness can lead to greater emotional resilience and improved mental clarity.

Additionally, the physical aspect of breathwork contributes to the benefits of yoga in somatic therapy. Breathing deeply allows for greater oxygen intake, which is vital for cellular health and energy production. As you practice, you may notice increased vitality and reduced fatigue. Moreover, the movement associated with breath in yoga poses enhances circulation and promotes the release of stored tension in the body.

Let's explore the benefits of breathwork and its progression:

Deep breathing lowers stress instantly.

Breath regulation calms the nervous system.

Breathwork helps process emotions.

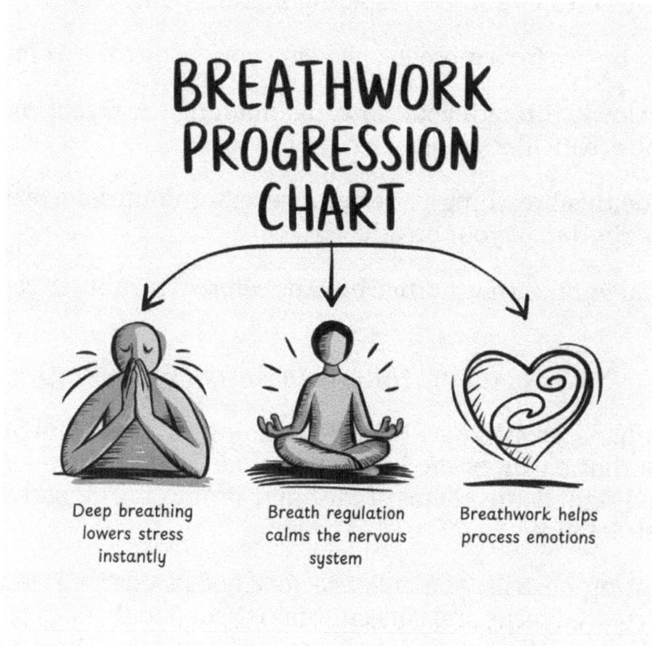

Ujjayi Pranayama (Ocean's Breath)

Ujjayi Pranayama is known as Ocean's Breath for its soothing sound, reminiscent of ocean waves. This technique calms the mind and reduces anxiety. By focusing on the breath, you enhance your mindfulness and cultivate a greater sense of presence.

Ujjayi encourages deeper breathing, increasing lung capacity and oxygen intake. This can invigorate your energy levels and enhance overall vitality. As you practice, the rhythmic sound of your breath promotes relaxation, helping to release tension in the body and mind.

Additionally, this breathing technique activates the parasympathetic nervous system. This system helps to calm the body and lower stress levels. Regular practice of Ujjayi can lead to improved emotional regulation and mental clarity, making it easier to navigate life's challenges.

How to Practice Ujjayi Pranayama:

1. Begin in a comfortable seated position with your spine straight and shoulders relaxed.

2. Close your eyes and take a few deep breaths through your nose, letting your abdomen expand on the inhale and contract on the exhale.

3. Inhale deeply through your nose, constricting the back of your throat slightly. This creates a soft, whispering sound as you breathe.

4. Hold the breath for a moment, allowing your body to relax further.

5. Exhale slowly through your nose, maintaining the throat constriction to keep the ocean-like sound.

6. Continue this breathing pattern for several minutes, focusing on the sound and rhythm of your breath.

7. To conclude, take a few normal breaths before returning to your regular breathing.

Nadi Shodhana (Alternate Nostril Breathing)

Nadi Shodhana, or Alternate Nostril Breathing, is a powerful pranayama technique that balances the body and mind. This practice harmonizes the left and right hemispheres of the brain, promoting mental clarity and emotional stability.

By alternating nostrils, you enhance your body's energy flow. This can lead to increased focus and concentration. Nadi Shodhana is particularly beneficial for reducing anxiety and stress. The rhythmic breathing calms the nervous system, helping you feel more centered and relaxed.

Practicing Nadi Shodhana can also improve respiratory function. This technique encourages deeper breaths, promoting greater lung capacity and oxygen intake. Improved breathing can enhance physical endurance and overall well-being.

Moreover, this practice fosters a sense of mindfulness. As you focus on your breath, you cultivate a deeper connection with yourself. This self-awareness can lead to greater emotional resilience, enabling you to navigate life's ups and downs with grace.

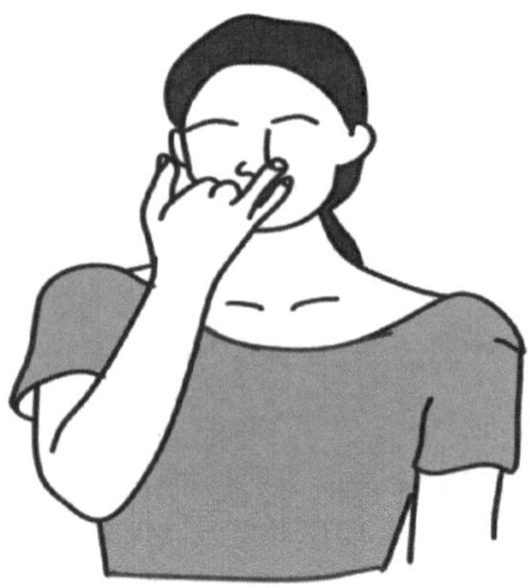

How to Practice Nadi Shodhana:

1. Sit comfortably with your spine straight and shoulders relaxed.

2. Close your right nostril with your right thumb.

3. Inhale deeply through your left nostril.

4. Close your left nostril with your right ring finger, and release your right nostril.

5. Exhale slowly through your right nostril.

6. Inhale through your right nostril, then close it with your right thumb.

7. Release your left nostril and exhale through it.

8. This completes one round. Continue this alternating pattern for several minutes.

CHAPTER 9
ENHANCING FOCUS AND CONCENTRATION

Yoga serves as an effective somatic therapy to enhance blood flow, focus, concentration, and memory. When you practice yoga, you encourage circulation throughout your body. Improved blood flow nourishes your organs and muscles. This increase in oxygen and nutrients helps your brain function more effectively.

As you move through yoga poses, you engage various muscle groups. This physical activity stimulates your cardiovascular system. As your body becomes more energized, so does your mind.

Breath control in yoga plays a crucial role. Techniques like Ujjayi or Nadi Shodhana help calm your mind. Focusing on your breath allows you to tune out distractionsWith regular practice, you may notice an improvement in your focus during daily tasks.

Certain poses target areas that promote concentration. For example, balancing poses like Vrikshasana (Tree Pose) and Garudasana (Eagle Pose) require mental awareness. These poses challenge your stability and encourage you to stay present. As you balance, you sharpen your mental acuity.

Vrikshasana (Tree Pose)

Vrikshasana, or Tree Pose, offers numerous benefits for both the body and mind. One of the primary advantages is its ability to promote balance and stability. Additionally, Tree Pose cultivates mental focus and concentration. By finding a steady point to gaze at, you encourage your mind to become anchored and present. This mindfulness practice can help reduce distractions and enhance your ability to concentrate on tasks at hand. As you become more adept at balancing, you may notice improvements in your mental clarity and decision-making skills.

Moreover, Vrikshasana is grounding. The act of rooting your foot into the earth while reaching upward creates a sense of stability. This grounding effect can be especially beneficial during times of stress or anxiety, helping you feel more centered and secure. The combination of grounding and reaching can harmonize your energy, promoting a sense of equilibrium.

How to Practice Vrikshasana:

1. Begin by standing tall in Tadasana (Mountain Pose) with your feet together.

2. Shift your weight onto your left foot, grounding it firmly into the earth.

3. Bend your right knee and bring your right foot to the inner thigh or calf of your left leg (avoid the knee).

4. Find a focal point in front of you to maintain balance.

5. Press your right foot into your left leg and your left leg into your right foot.

6. As you inhale, raise your arms overhead, palms together or arms parallel, reaching toward the sky.

7. Hold the pose for several breaths, feeling the stability in your standing leg and the length in your spine.

8. To release, lower your arms and gently bring your right foot back to the floor. Switch sides and repeat.

Benefits:

Incorporating Vrikshasana into your yoga practice can also enhance your physical strength. The muscles in your standing leg engage to support your weight, building endurance and stability. This pose can lead to improved posture and alignment as you develop greater strength in your legs and core.

Conclusion:

Practicing Vrikshasana regularly allows you to cultivate balance, concentration, and grounding energy. By connecting with your body and breath in this pose, you can enhance your overall well-being. Embrace the power of Tree Pose to foster resilience and presence in your daily life.

Prasarita Padottanasana (Wide-Legged Forward Bend)

Prasarita Padottanasana, or Wide-Legged Forward Bend, offers numerous benefits that encourage mental clarity and grounding. This pose allows for deep stretching in the hamstrings and lower back, helping to relieve tension and fatigue.

The release of tension in the back and hamstrings during this pose can also alleviate feelings of anxiety or stress. As you breathe deeply, you allow oxygen to flow into your body, invigorating your mind and spirit. This combination of physical release and mental clarity can create a powerful sense of empowerment and resilience.

How to Practice Prasarita Padottanasana:

1. Begin standing with your feet wide apart, about four to five feet, depending on your flexibility.

2. Turn your toes slightly inward and ensure your heels are in line with your feet.

3. Inhale deeply, reaching your arms overhead to lengthen your spine.

4. As you exhale, hinge at your hips and fold forward, bringing your hands to the floor or onto blocks.

5. Keep your back flat and your head relaxed as you lower yourself.

6. Hold the pose for several breaths, allowing your head to hang heavy and your spine to release.

7. To exit, engage your core as you slowly rise back to standing, using your hands for support if needed.

BOOK 5

Toolbox

Key Takeaway Points

Overview of Somatic Therapy

- Definition: Somatic therapy is a holistic approach to healing that focuses on the connection between the mind and body.

- Core Principle: It recognizes that emotional experiences often manifest physically.

- Goal: The goal is to help individuals process and release trauma stored in the body, promoting overall well-being.

- Approach: Somatic therapy integrates body awareness with psychological techniques, allowing for deeper emotional healing.

- Mind-Body Connection: Understanding the link between physical sensations and emotional states is essential for healing.

- Emotional Awareness: Somatic therapy encourages individuals to become aware of their bodily sensations and how these relate to emotions.

- Holistic Healing: It addresses both physical and psychological aspects of trauma, making it a comprehensive form of therapy.

- Personal Empowerment: By learning to listen to your body, you can gain insight into your emotional experiences and promote self-healing.

- Physiological Basis: Somatic therapy is grounded in scientific principles of psychology and physiology.

- Nervous System: Trauma can affect the nervous system, leading to dysregulation. Somatic therapy helps reset the nervous system.

- Neuroscience: Research shows that body-based interventions can positively impact emotional regulation and mental health.

- Body Memory: The body can store traumatic memories. Somatic therapy helps release these memories through physical practices.

Working with Trauma in the Body

- Trauma Storage: Trauma can be stored in various parts of the body, affecting physical and emotional well-being.

- Creating Safety: It's crucial to create a safe environment for individuals to explore their trauma through bodily sensations.

- Body Awareness: Somatic practices encourage awareness of where trauma is held in the body, allowing for gradual release.

- Processing Experiences: Techniques like movement, breathwork, and touch can facilitate the processing of traumatic experiences.

Grounding and Self-Regulation Techniques

- Grounding Techniques: Grounding exercises help individuals connect with their bodies and the present moment.

- Sensory Awareness: Engaging the senses (sight, sound, touch) promotes self-regulation and emotional stability.

The Role of Breathwork in Somatic Therapy

- Breath as a Tool: Breathwork is a central component of somatic therapy, facilitating emotional release.

- Types of Breathwork: Techniques include diaphragmatic breathing and conscious connected breathing.

- Emotional Release: Regulating the breath can help individuals access and process deep emotions.

- Relaxation and Calm: Breathwork promotes relaxation and can reduce symptoms of anxiety and stress.

Movement and Expressive Practices

- Physical Expression: Movement allows individuals to express emotions that may be difficult to verbalize.

- Dance and Movement: Dance, yoga, and other forms of movement can release pent-up emotions and foster body awareness.

- Expressive Arts: Creative practices, like painting or drawing, can complement somatic therapy by encouraging self-expression.

The Power of Visualization and Guided Imagery

- Visualization Techniques: Guided imagery can enhance the therapeutic process by promoting healing.

- Mental Safe Spaces: Creating mental images of safety and calm can help individuals manage anxiety and stress.

- Fostering Positive Emotions: Visualization can lead to the cultivation of positive emotions and coping strategies.

Creativity and Play in Somatic Healing

- Role of Creativity: Engaging in creative activities fosters self-expression and emotional exploration.

- Artistic Practices: Activities such as drawing, music, and writing can be therapeutic and help process feelings.

Yoga and Somatic Therapy

- Fundamentals of Yoga: Yoga offers numerous benefits for the mind and body, promoting healing through movement and breath.

- Synergy with Somatic Therapy: Integrating yoga into somatic therapy enhances body awareness and emotional processing.

- Stress Relief through Yoga: Specific yoga poses and breathwork techniques are effective for reducing stress and promoting relaxation.

- Managing Anxiety: Calming yoga poses help create a sense of safety and reduce anxiety symptoms.

- Meditation in Yoga: Incorporating meditation into yoga practice enhances mindfulness and emotional regulation.

- Energizing Practices: Certain yoga sequences can invigorate the body and increase mental alertness.

- Alleviating Depression: Restorative yoga practices can uplift mood and support emotional healing.

- Breath Awareness: Breath regulation is central to yoga practice, enhancing breath awareness and emotional balance.

- Focus and Concentration: Yoga practices can improve focus and concentration, fostering present-moment awareness.

- Developing a Personal Practice: Establishing a consistent, personalized yoga practice supports growth and emotional healing.

JOURNALING PROMPTS

Journaling is a powerful tool in somatic therapy that fosters self-reflection and emotional awareness. By putting thoughts and feelings into words, you can deepen your understanding of the mind body connection and explore how physical sensations relate to emotional experiences. This practice encourages you to observe patterns, identify triggers, and process complex emotions. Journaling can also help ground you in the present moment, enhancing your ability to self-regulate and engage with your bodily sensations. You will find ten prompts designed to facilitate your journey through somatic therapy and cultivate greater self-awareness.

1. Describe Your Current Physical Sensations

Take a moment to close your eyes and tune into your body. What sensations do you feel? Notice any areas of tension, warmth, or discomfort. Write about these sensations in detail. Where do you feel them in your body? Are there any specific emotions or memories that come to mind when you focus on these sensations? Reflect on how these feelings impact your overall mood and emotional state. This exercise can help you connect physical sensations to underlying emotional experiences, fostering greater awareness of your mind-body connection.

2. Reflect on a Recent Emotional Experience

Think back to a recent emotional experience that stood out to you. Write about the event in detail, focusing on how it made you feel physically. Did you notice any changes in your body, such as tension, heaviness, or lightness? Explore the emotions that arose during this experience. How did these emotions manifest in your body? Were there any specific thoughts or beliefs that contributed to how you felt? Reflecting on this experience can help you identify patterns and deepen your understanding of your emotional responses.

3. Identify Your Triggers

Take a moment to consider situations or experiences that trigger strong emotional or physical reactions. Write down specific triggers and the emotions they evoke. What physical sensations accompany these feelings? Reflect on how you typically respond to these triggers and whether your reactions are helpful or unhelpful. Consider how you can use your awareness of these triggers in the future to create a more grounded response. Understanding your triggers can enhance your emotional regulation and support your somatic therapy journey.

4. Explore Your Coping Mechanisms

Write about the ways you cope with stress and difficult emotions. What strategies do you typically use to manage these feelings? Are your coping mechanisms healthy and supportive, or do they contribute to further discomfort? Reflect on how these strategies impact your physical body. For example, do you find yourself tensing up, holding your breath, or engaging in other physical responses? This exploration can help you identify patterns in your coping mechanisms and consider healthier alternatives that align with somatic practices.

5. Visualize a Safe Space

Imagine a safe and calming space where you feel completely at ease. Describe this place in detail, focusing on the sensory experiences it provides. What do you see, hear, smell, and feel? Write about the emotions that arise when you visualize this space. How does it feel in your body to imagine being there? Use this visualization as a tool for grounding when you feel overwhelmed. Reflect on how you can incorporate this safe space into your daily life to support your emotional well-being.

6. Body Scan Reflection

Perform a body scan, starting from the top of your head and moving down to your toes. Pay attention to each body part, noticing any sensations, tension, or areas of relaxation. Write about your experience during the body scan. Were there any areas that felt particularly tense or relaxed? Did any emotions or memories surface while focusing on specific parts of your body? Reflecting on your body scan can help you cultivate awareness of physical sensations and their connection to emotional states.

7. Describe Your Ideal Emotional State

Reflect on what your ideal emotional state would look and feel like. How would you feel in your body if you were experiencing this state? Write about the sensations, energy levels, and overall mood that come to mind. Consider the activities or practices that help you achieve this state. What grounding techniques, breathwork, or movement practices support your emotional well-being? Visualizing your ideal state can help you identify strategies to cultivate these feelings in your daily life.

8. The Role of Movement in Your Life

Write about the role movement plays in your emotional and physical well-being. What types of movement do you enjoy? How does movement impact your mood and stress levels? Reflect on how you can incorporate more intentional movement into your life. Consider exploring different forms of movement, such as yoga, dance, or walking in nature. Writing about your relationship with movement can enhance your awareness of its importance in your somatic therapy journey and support emotional regulation.

9. Create a Gratitude List

Take a moment to reflect on the things you are grateful for in your life. Write down at least ten items, focusing on both small and significant aspects. How do these things make you feel in your body? Do they evoke warmth, joy, or relaxation? Gratitude can help shift your emotional state and promote positive feelings. Consider how incorporating gratitude practices into your daily routine can enhance your somatic therapy journey and overall well-being.

10. Reflect on Your Progress

Take time to reflect on your journey through somatic therapy. Write about the changes you have noticed in your body, emotions, and overall well-being. What have you learned about yourself? How has your relationship with your body evolved? Consider the challenges you've faced and the progress you've made. Reflecting on your journey can provide valuable insight into your healing process and help reinforce your commitment to continued growth and self-discovery.

ASTROCARTOGRAPHY RESOURCE GUIDE

An Introduction to Astrocartotherapy

Astrocartography is a specialized branch of astrology that maps the influence of celestial bodies on different geographical locations. By creating a personalized astrocartography map based on a person's natal chart, this technique reveals where planetary energies are strongest around the world. Each planet is associated with specific qualities—such as love, creativity, ambition, and conflict—which influence the environment in different locations. For example, a Venus line might enhance relationships and harmony, while a Mars line may amplify assertiveness and challenges. Understanding these planetary energies can empower individuals to make informed decisions about where to travel, live, or work, aligning their surroundings with their personal growth and emotional well-being.

Astrocartotherapy integrates astrocartography with somatic therapy to offer a holistic approach to healing. Somatic therapy focuses on the body's role in emotional and psychological healing by bringing attention to physical sensations and their connection to emotions. By merging the two practices, astrocartotherapy explores how the energy of different locations interacts with the body's sensations and emotional states. This fusion aims to deepen self-awareness, promote emotional regulation, and enhance physical and mental well-being by leveraging the unique influences of geographical spaces.

The Principles Behind Astrocartography and Somatic Therapy

Astrocartography is based on the understanding that the positions and movements of celestial bodies can influence different geographic areas, creating energy lines that reflect these effects. These lines—each representing a different planet—show where the energy of that planet is felt most strongly. For instance:

Venus Line: A place for love, creativity, and harmonious relationships.

Mars Line: A location that may bring challenges, conflict, or assertiveness.

Jupiter Line: Places associated with growth, abundance, and expansive opportunities.

Saturn Line: Locations that may bring discipline, structure, and hard lessons.

Somatic therapy, on the other hand, involves techniques that bring attention to the body's sensations, such as breathwork, movement, and mindfulness. These practices acknowledge that emotions are often stored in the body and that healing occurs by releasing physical tension and connecting with sensations. Integrating these two practices allows individuals to explore the physical and emotional impact of different locations and use somatic techniques to engage with the energy of those places.

How Astrocartotherapy Enhances Personal Growth and Healing

By combining the insights from astrocartography and somatic therapy, astrocartotherapy provides a more comprehensive approach to self-exploration and healing. Locations on your astrocartography map can influence your emotions and physical responses, helping you identify places where you might thrive or experience challenges. This awareness creates opportunities for personal growth by allowing you to engage in healing practices tailored to the energies of specific locations.

For example:

Supportive Locations: If your Venus line runs through a city, it may be an excellent place for cultivating relationships or pursuing creative endeavors. By aligning somatic practices—such as movement or breathwork—with the supportive energies of Venus, you can deepen your connection with love and creativity.

Challenging Locations: A Mars line may indicate areas that bring conflict or stress. In such locations, somatic practices that promote grounding and relaxation can help you navigate the heightened energy with more ease and resilience.

Astrocartotherapy not only helps identify where to travel or live but also empowers you to navigate your emotional and physical landscapes by understanding the energy patterns of different places. It brings attention to how geographical influences impact your body, emotions, and overall state of well-being, offering you new tools for emotional regulation and growth.

Practical Applications of Astrocartotherapy

Personalized Somatic Practices: By analyzing your astrocartography map, you can tailor somatic therapy techniques to align with the energies of specific locations. For instance, in a place influenced by your Jupiter line (growth and expansion), you might focus on expansive practices such as deep breathwork or dynamic movement. Alternatively, when in a challenging location tied to a Mars line, grounding exercises and relaxation techniques can help manage any tension or stress.

Self-Reflection and Awareness: The integration of astrocartography encourages deep self-reflection. By exploring how certain locations make you feel or influence your body's responses, you can develop a better understanding of the emotions and sensations that arise in specific environments. This self-awareness fosters emotional regulation and helps you make conscious decisions about where to spend time or settle.

Tailoring Healing to Locations: During your somatic therapy sessions, your therapist may guide you through exercises that reflect the energy of a location on your astrocartography map. For example, if you are near a location aligned with your Sun line (identity and self-expression), your session may focus on building confidence and self-empowerment. If you're near a Neptune line (spirituality and intuition), the session might incorporate meditation or creative practices that connect you to your inner wisdom.

Astrocartography and Mindfulness: Mindfulness practices, when combined with astrocartography, can further enhance your emotional and physical connection to different places.

The Integration of Astrocartography and Somatic Therapy for a Holistic Approach to Healing

Astrocartography and somatic therapy work synergistically to provide a holistic framework for healing. This integration helps you create a personalized map of healing that incorporates both your physical body and the energy of different places. Whether you are seeking personal growth, emotional healing, or physical relaxation, astrocartotherapy offers a way to align your surroundings with your personal needs.

By understanding the planetary influences of specific locations, you can tailor your somatic practices to enhance your well-being. This combination encourages a more profound connection to yourself and your environment, creating a space for self-discovery, emotional balance, and healing.

Astrocartotherapy offers a unique opportunity for growth by integrating the ancient wisdom of astrology with modern somatic practices. It allows you to harness the power of geography, aligning your journey toward healing and self-discovery with the cosmic energies that influence your life.

Planetary Lines and Meanings

Astrocartography maps display various planetary lines, each associated with different energies and influences that can significantly impact personal experiences. Here's a breakdown of the key planetary lines and their meanings:

1. Sun Line: The Sun represents vitality, self-expression, and purpose. Locations along the Sun line can boost confidence and illuminate one's path in life, often leading to personal growth and fulfillment.

2. Moon Line: The Moon governs emotions, intuition, and family connections. Places along this line may enhance emotional awareness and provide comfort, making them ideal for nurturing relationships or personal reflection.

3. Mercury Line: Mercury influences communication, intellect, and adaptability. Locations along this line can enhance cognitive abilities and facilitate learning, making them suitable for educational pursuits or networking opportunities.

4. Venus Line: Associated with love, beauty, and creativity, the Venus line can enhance romantic relationships and artistic endeavors. Being in a location along this line may foster harmony and connection with others.

5. Mars Line: Mars embodies action, energy, and assertiveness. Locations along the Mars line may bring challenges, conflict, or heightened motivation. These areas can be empowering for individuals seeking to pursue goals but may also evoke stress or tension.

6. Jupiter Line: The planet of expansion and abundance, Jupiter's line indicates locations where opportunities for growth and success are heightened. These areas can promote optimism, adventure, and new experiences.

7. Saturn Line: Saturn represents discipline, structure, and responsibility. Being near a Saturn line may lead to challenges, but it also provides opportunities for personal development and mastery over one's life.

8. Uranus Line: Associated with innovation and change, the Uranus line can bring sudden shifts and new ideas. These locations may foster creativity and encourage individuals to break free from routine.

9. Neptune Line: Neptune influences dreams, intuition, and spirituality. Locations along this line may enhance creativity and spiritual experiences but can also lead to confusion or disillusionment.

10. Pluto Line: Pluto represents transformation, power, and intensity. Being in areas associated with Pluto may bring deep personal change and a sense of renewal but can also evoke intense emotions or challenges.

In addition to understanding planetary lines, it's essential to consider how astrocartography insights can be used practically. When planning travel or relocation, individuals can reflect on how the energies of specific locations align with their goals. For instance, someone seeking a fresh start might look for opportunities along their Jupiter line, while someone focused on healing might explore their Moon line locations for emotional support.

Journaling can also be a valuable practice when engaging with astrocartography. Individuals can document their experiences in various locations, noting how they felt physically and emotionally in relation to the planetary lines present. This reflective practice can help deepen the understanding of how geography affects personal experiences.

Finally, consider creating a vision board that combines astrocartography insights with personal goals. Use images and affirmations related to the qualities associated with specific planetary

lines to manifest your desired experiences in those locations. This creative approach reinforces the connection between location, energy, and personal healing, making the astrocartotherapy process both insightful and transformative.

Creating and Understanding Your Astrocartography Map (1000 words)

Creating your astrocartography map is the first in exploring the geographical influences on your life. Follow these steps to generate your map:

1. Gather Information: You will need your birth date, time, and location. Accurate birth information is crucial for generating a precise natal chart.

2. Use Online Tools: Several websites and software programs offer free astrocartography mapping services. Popular options include Astro.com and Astrodienst. Navigate to their astrocartography section and enter your birth details.

3. Generate the Map: Once you've entered your information, the site will create your natal chart along with an astrocartography map. This map will display various planetary lines across the globe.

4. Analyze the Map: Look for the key planetary lines—each associated with different energies and influences. Identify where these lines intersect your locations of interest. This will help you understand which areas may support or challenge your emotional and physical experiences.

5. Print and Mark: Print your astrocartography map and mark significant locations where you've lived, traveled, or are considering. This visual representation can assist in making informed decisions about future travels or relocations.

DAILY PLANNER

Welcome to your Daily Planner for somatic therapy! This planner serves as a guide to help you integrate grounding, emotional regulation, anxiety and stress management, and trauma recovery practices into your daily life.

Engaging in somatic exercises can significantly enhance your overall well-being by fostering a deeper connection to your body, promoting emotional awareness, and encouraging self-compassion. By dedicating time each day to these practices, you create space for healing, resilience, and personal growth.

As you go through and follow this planner, remember that healing is not a linear process. Be gentle with yourself and allow for fluctuations in your journey.

As you embark on this four-week exploration, here are some tips to make the most of your daily planner:

- Establish a Consistent Time:

Set aside a regular time for your exercises that fits your lifestyle. Consistency will reinforce the importance of these practices in your daily routine.

- Create a Dedicated Space:

Designate a specific area for your activities, whether it's a cozy corner in your home or a peaceful outdoor setting. An intentional environment can enhance your focus and make your practice more enjoyable.

- Keep an Open Mind and Heart:

Approach each exercise with curiosity and openness. Allow yourself to feel whatever arises without judgment, embracing this journey as a valuable opportunity for self-discovery and healing.

Feel free to adjust any of the points to better fit your needs!

Week 1: Grounding Exercises

We will start by exploring grounding exercises designed to help you connect with the present moment and foster a sense of stability. Grounding techniques are essential for cultivating mindfulness and enhancing your awareness of the physical sensations in your body. By focusing on the here and now, you can create a solid foundation for managing overwhelming emotions and reducing anxiety. Each day, we'll engage in a different grounding practice that encourages you to anchor yourself in your surroundings, nurture self-awareness, and cultivate a deeper connection to your body. As you embark on this week of exploration, allow yourself to be open to the sensations and experiences that arise, fostering a greater sense of peace and presence in your daily life.

Day 1: Breath Awareness

Today, we will focus on Breath Awareness. This exercise is a fundamental grounding technique that helps anchor you in the present moment. Begin by finding a comfortable position—either sitting or lying down. Close your eyes gently and take a deep breath in through your nose, allowing your belly to expand. Hold that breath for a moment, then slowly exhale through your mouth. As you breathe, pay attention to the sensations in your body: the rise and fall of your chest, the coolness of the air entering your nostrils, and the warmth of your exhale. If your mind begins to wander, acknowledge those thoughts and gently bring your focus back to your breath. Continue this practice for several minutes, allowing each inhale to fill you with calm and each exhale to release tension. Afterward, take a moment to reflect on how this practice makes you feel. Write down any thoughts or sensations that arise during this exercise in your journal. This will help reinforce your experience and serve as a reminder of your capacity to ground yourself through Fbreath.

Day 2: Body Scan

Today's exercise is the Body Scan, a powerful tool for connecting with your physical self and noticing sensations without judgment. Find a quiet space where you can either lie down or sit comfortably. Close your eyes and take a few deep breaths to settle into the moment. Begin at the top of your head, directing your attention to that area. Notice any sensations, tension, or relaxation. Slowly move your awareness down through your forehead, cheeks, and jaw, acknowledging any feelings you encounter. Continue scanning down your neck, shoulders, arms, and torso, observing each part of your body in turn. As you reach your legs and feet, note any areas of discomfort or relaxation. If you encounter tension, visualize your breath flowing to that area, inviting it to soften and release. This exercise encourages you to be present with your body and its sensations. After completing the scan, reflect on your experience. What did you notice? Were there areas of tension or relaxation that surprised you? Jot down your reflections in your journal to deepen your awareness of your physical state.

Day 3: Five Senses Exercise

For today's grounding practice, we will engage in the Five Senses Exercise. This activity invites you to connect with your environment and sharpen your awareness of the present moment. Begin by finding a comfortable space where you can focus without distractions. Take a few deep breaths to center yourself. Now, start with your sight: look around you and identify five things you can see. They can be as simple as the color of the walls, a plant, or a shadow. Next, move on to touch: find four things you can physically touch, like the fabric of your clothing or a textured object nearby. Then, listen carefully for three sounds—these could be distant noises or sounds within the room. Shift your focus to your smell and identify two scents in your environment. Finally, focus on your taste and notice one flavor, whether it's lingering from a recent meal or the freshness of the air. This exercise grounds you by engaging all your senses, drawing your awareness to the present. Afterward, take a moment to reflect on your experience and how it felt to be fully present in your surroundings.

Day 4: Grounding Visualization

Today's exercise is a Grounding Visualization. This technique helps you connect to the earth and cultivate a sense of stability and support. Find a comfortable position, either sitting or lying down, in a quiet space. Close your eyes and take a few deep breaths, allowing your body to relax. Now, imagine roots growing from the soles of your feet, extending deep into the earth. Visualize these roots anchoring you securely, drawing strength and nourishment from the ground below. Picture the earth's energy flowing through your roots and into your body, filling you with warmth and stability. As you breathe, feel this energy supporting you, reminding you that you are safe and connected. Spend a few moments in this visualization, focusing on the sensations of strength and grounding. When you're ready, gently bring your awareness back to the room. Open your eyes and take a moment to reflect on your experience. How did it feel to visualize this connection? Write about any insights or sensations that arose during the exercise.

Day 5: Nature Connection

Today, we'll explore Nature Connection as a grounding exercise. Spending time in nature can be incredibly restorative and help you feel more present in your body. If possible, find a nearby park, garden, or natural area. As you outside, take a moment to pause and notice your surroundings. Engage your senses: feel the ground beneath your feet, notice the colors of the leaves, and listen to the sounds of birds or wind. As you walk, pay attention to the sensations of the air on your skin and the warmth of the sun or coolness of the shade. If you prefer to stay indoors, you can bring nature inside by placing a plant near you or looking out a window. Take time to connect with this natural element. Reflect on how being in nature makes you feel. What thoughts or emotions arise? Write down your reflections, noting how this connection to the earth can help ground you during challenging moments.

Day 6: Walking Meditation

For today's practice, we'll engage in Walking Meditation, a mindful way to ground yourself while moving. Find a quiet space where you can walk comfortably without distractions. Start by standing still, taking a moment to connect with your breath. As you begin to walk, pay close attention to the sensations in your feet and legs. Notice how your feet touch the ground, how your weight shifts, and the rhythm of your movement. Walk slowly and mindfully, focusing on each step. If your mind starts to wander, gently redirect your attention back to the sensations of walking. You can also incorporate your surroundings by noticing the sights, sounds, and smells around you as you walk. This exercise allows you to ground yourself through movement, connecting your mind and body. After your walking meditation, take a moment to reflect on your experience. How did it feel to walk mindfully? What sensations or thoughts did you notice? Jot down your insights in your journal to reinforce this practice.

Day 7: Tactile Grounding

Today's grounding exercise is Tactile Grounding, which utilizes physical touch to bring your awareness back to the present.

Begin by selecting a small object that you can hold in your hand. This could be a smooth stone, a piece of fabric, or a stress ball. Find a comfortable space to sit or stand. Close your eyes and take a few deep breaths to center yourself.

Hold the object and focus on its texture, weight, and temperature. Notice how it feels against your skin and in your palm. As you explore the object, allow yourself to be fully present in the moment.

If your mind starts to drift, gently bring your attention back to the sensations you're experiencing. You might even want to describe the object to yourself, paying attention to its details. This exercise helps you anchor yourself in the here and now through the sense of touch.

Afterward, take a moment to reflect on your experience and write about it in your journal. How did this tactile focus affect your awareness and grounding?

Week 2: Managing Emotions

In Week 2, we shift our focus to managing emotions through a variety of exercises designed to help you identify, process, and express your feelings in a healthy way. Understanding your emotions is crucial for emotional regulation and overall well-being. Throughout this week, you will engage in daily practices that encourage introspection and creative expression, allowing you to explore the depths of your emotional landscape. From journaling and creative expression to mindful breathing, each exercise is intended to provide you with tools to cultivate emotional resilience. As you navigate this week, embrace the opportunity to deepen your understanding of your emotions, fostering compassion for yourself and the experiences that shape you.

Day 1: Journaling

Today, we'll explore Journaling as a way to manage emotions. Journaling is a powerful tool for self-reflection and emotional processing. Set aside a quiet space where you can write freely without distractions. Begin by taking a few deep breaths to center yourself. Open your journal and write about your current emotions. What are you feeling right now? Try to describe your emotions in detail, including any physical sensations you notice in your body. Ask yourself questions like: What triggered these feelings? How do they manifest in my thoughts or actions? Allow your thoughts to flow onto the page without worrying about grammar or structure. This exercise is not about creating a perfect entry; it's about expressing yourself authentically. After writing, take a moment to reflect on your entry. What insights did you gain about your emotions? How can you apply this understanding in your daily life? Journaling regularly can help you track emotional patterns, identify triggers, and develop healthier responses to your feelings.

Day 2: Emotion Wheel

Today, we'll use the Emotion Wheel to deepen our understanding of our emotions. The Emotion Wheel is a visual tool that categorizes feelings, helping you identify and articulate what you're experiencing. Begin by finding or drawing your own Emotion Wheel, which includes primary emotions like joy, sadness, anger, and fear, along with more nuanced feelings. Take a few moments to sit quietly and check in with yourself. What emotions are you feeling today? Locate these feelings on the wheel and explore their nuances. Choose one emotion to focus on and write about it in your journal. Consider the triggers that led to this feeling and any physical sensations associated with it. Reflect on how this emotion affects your thoughts and behaviors. Engaging with the Emotion Wheel allows you to better articulate your feelings and recognize that it's okay to experience a range of emotions. By identifying and acknowledging your feelings, you can develop a deeper emotional awareness and healthier coping strategies in response to them.

Day 3: Physical Movement

For today's practice, we'll engage in Physical Movement to express and manage emotions. Physical activity is a powerful way to release pent-up energy and emotions. Choose a form of movement that resonates with you—this could be dancing, yoga, or even a brisk walk. Begin by warming up your body with some gentle stretches or a short walk to get your blood flowing. As you move, pay attention to the emotions that arise. If you feel tension or frustration, allow that energy to manifest in your movements. Dance freely to music, stretch deeply, or practice yoga poses that feel good to your body. You might also want to shake out any feelings of stress or negativity. After your movement session, take a few moments to reflect on your experience. What emotions did you notice during the practice? How did your body respond to those feelings? Write down your reflections in your journal, acknowledging the connection between your physical state and emotional well-being.

Day 4: Mindful Breathing

Today, we'll practice Mindful Breathing to create space for emotional awareness. Mindful breathing is a simple yet effective technique that helps you remain present with your emotions. Find a quiet place to sit comfortably. Close your eyes and take a deep breath in through your nose, feeling your belly expand. Hold the breath for a moment, then exhale slowly through your mouth. As you breathe, focus your attention on the rhythm of your breath. If a strong emotion arises, acknowledge it without judgment. You might silently repeat a phrase like, "I am feeling this emotion" as you breathe in and out. This practice encourages you to observe your feelings from a distance rather than being overwhelmed by them. Continue this mindful breathing for several minutes, allowing each breath to help you stay centered. Afterward, reflect on how this practice influenced your awareness of your emotions. Did you notice any shifts or changes? Write about your experience in your journal, reinforcing the connection between mindful breathing and emotional regulation.

Day 5: Creative Expression

For today's exercise, we'll explore Creative Expression as a way to manage emotions. Engaging in creative activities can provide an outlet for feelings that are difficult to articulate. Choose a medium that resonates with you, whether it's drawing, painting, writing, or making music. Set aside dedicated time for this activity without distractions. Start by taking a few deep breaths to center yourself. Then, allow your emotions to guide your creative process. If you feel sad, use dark colors or write about your feelings; if you're feeling joyful, let bright colors or uplifting melodies flow. The key is to express your emotions authentically, without worrying about the final product. After your creative session, take a moment to reflect on what you created. How did the process make you feel? Did you uncover any insights about your emotions through your art? Jot down your reflections in your journal, noting the power of creativity in emotional expression and healing.

Day 6: Check-in with the Body

Today's practice involves a Check-in with the Body to explore where emotions manifest physically. Begin by finding a quiet, comfortable space to sit or lie down. Close your eyes and take a few deep breaths, bringing your awareness inward. Start by scanning your body from head to toe, paying attention to any sensations, tensions, or areas of discomfort.

Notice where you hold emotions—perhaps you feel tightness in your chest when anxious or tension in your shoulders when stressed. Once you've identified these areas, place a hand on the spot that feels the most intense and take a few slow breaths into that area. Allow yourself to be present with those sensations, acknowledging the emotions connected to them without judgment. After this check-in, reflect on your experience. What did you notice about the relationship between your body and emotions? Write down your insights in your journal, deepening your understanding of how emotions are experienced physically.

Day 7: Affirmations

For our final exercise this week, we'll practice Affirmations to cultivate positive emotions and resilience. Affirmations are positive statements that can help shift your mindset and reinforce your emotional well-being. Begin by finding a quiet space to sit comfortably. Take a few deep breaths to center yourself. Reflect on the emotions you want to nurture, such as self-love, confidence, or resilience. Create a list of affirmations that resonate with you, such as "I am worthy of love" or "I have the strength to face my challenges." Repeat these affirmations aloud or silently to yourself, allowing their meaning to sink in. Consider incorporating these affirmations into your daily routine—perhaps saying them in the morning or writing them down in your journal. As you continue this practice, pay attention to how it influences your emotions and mindset. Reflect on your experience and write down any changes you notice in your emotional state throughout the week. Affirmations can be a powerful tool in managing emotions and fostering a positive self-image.

Week 3: Anxiety and Stress Management

In this week, we will focus on anxiety and stress management techniques. Life can often feel overwhelming, and learning to cope with anxiety is essential for maintaining balance and well-being.

This week, we will explore various exercises aimed at calming the mind and body, promoting relaxation, and creating space for mindfulness. Each day, you will engage in practices that encourage you to identify stressors, implement calming strategies, and reconnect with your breath.

By incorporating these exercises into your routine, you will develop a toolkit to help navigate anxiety and stress effectively. Embrace this journey of self-discovery as you cultivate inner peace and resilience in the face of life's challenges.

Day 1: Progressive Muscle Relaxation

Today, we'll practice Progressive Muscle Relaxation (PMR) to manage anxiety and stress. This technique involves tensing and then relaxing different muscle groups in your body, promoting physical and mental relaxation. Find a quiet, comfortable space to sit or lie down. Begin by taking a few deep breaths, allowing your body to settle. Start with your feet: tense the muscles for a count of five, then release and notice the difference. Move to your calves, thighs, and so on, working your way up your body to your neck and face. As you tense each muscle group, focus on how the tension feels; when you relax, imagine letting go of all stress. This exercise not only reduces physical tension but also helps you become aware of areas in your body where you hold anxiety. After completing the practice, take a moment to reflect on how your body feels. Did you notice any significant changes? Write about your experience in your journal, reinforcing the connection between physical relaxation and emotional calm.

Day 2: Mindfulness Meditation

Today's practice focuses on Mindfulness Meditation as a way to manage anxiety and stress. This meditation encourages you to remain present and aware of your thoughts and feelings without judgment. Find a quiet space where you won't be disturbed. Sit comfortably, close your eyes, and take a few deep breaths. Bring your attention to your breath—notice the inhalation and exhalation, the sensations in your nostrils, and the rise and fall of your belly. As thoughts arise, acknowledge them without getting caught up in them. Gently guide your attention back to your breath. Start with just a few minutes, gradually increasing the time as you feel comfortable. This practice can help you cultivate a sense of calm and clarity, reducing feelings of anxiety. After your meditation, take a moment to reflect on your experience. What thoughts or feelings arose? How did your body respond during the practice? Write down your insights in your journal, emphasizing the benefits of mindfulness in managing anxiety.

Day 3: Nature Sounds

For today's exercise, we'll listen to Nature Sounds to create a calming atmosphere. Nature sounds, such as rain, ocean waves, or birds chirping, can significantly reduce stress and promote relaxation. Find a quiet place to sit comfortably and choose a nature sound recording that resonates with you. Close your eyes and take a few deep breaths to center yourself. As you listen to the sounds, allow them to wash over you. Focus on the details—notice the rhythm, pitch, and layers of the sounds. Imagine being in that natural setting, feeling the air, and experiencing the sights around you. As you immerse yourself in these sounds, pay attention to how your body responds. Notice any areas of tension releasing and a sense of calm settling in. After the listening session, reflect on your experience. How did the nature sounds affect your mood and stress levels? Write down your thoughts and any sensations you felt during the exercise.

Day 4: Visualization for Calm

Today, we'll engage in a Visualization for Calm to help reduce anxiety. Visualization is a powerful technique that uses your imagination to create a peaceful mental space. Find a comfortable, quiet spot to sit or lie down. Close your eyes and take several deep breaths to center yourself. Picture a serene place that brings you peace—a beach, a forest, or a quiet meadow. Visualize the details: the colors, the sounds, the scents, and how it feels to be there. Imagine the warmth of the sun or the coolness of the breeze. Allow this peaceful imagery to wash over you, replacing feelings of anxiety with calmness. Stay in this visualization for several minutes, allowing your mind to fully experience the tranquility of this space. When you're ready, gently bring your awareness back to the present moment. Reflect on your experience: How did this visualization impact your mood? Write down your thoughts in your journal, noting the effectiveness of imagery in managing anxiety.

Day 5: Gratitude List

For today's practice, we'll create a Gratitude List to help shift focus from stress to positivity. Gratitude is a powerful antidote to anxiety, encouraging a mindset of abundance rather than scarcity. Find a quiet space where you can reflect and write comfortably. Take a few deep breaths to center yourself, then list three things you are grateful for today. These can be big or small—anything from a supportive friend to a delicious meal. As you write, take time to reflect on why you're grateful for each item and how it makes you feel. Allow yourself to fully experience the positive emotions that arise as you focus on gratitude. You might even want to expand this exercise by reflecting on how these things have impacted your life positively. Afterward, take a moment to read over your list and notice any shifts in your mood. Write about your experience in your journal, emphasizing the role of gratitude in reducing anxiety and stress.

Day 6: Time-out Techniques

Today's exercise involves using Time-out Techniques to manage anxiety and stress. Taking short breaks throughout your day can significantly improve your well-being and reduce overwhelm. Identify moments in your day when you feel stressed or anxious. When these feelings arise, take a time-out. Find a quiet place where you can sit or stand for a moment. Engage in a brief activity that helps you reset—this could be a short walk, deep breathing, stretching, or sipping a cup of tea. Allow yourself to step away from stressors and recharge. During your time-out, pay attention to your body and mind. What sensations are you feeling? How does your mood shift after the break? When you return to your tasks, notice if you feel more centered and focused. Afterward, write about your experience in your journal, reflecting on the importance of taking breaks to manage anxiety and stress effectively.

Day 7: Breathing Techniques

For our final exercise this week, we'll practice various Breathing Techniques to promote relaxation and reduce anxiety. Deep, intentional breathing can help calm the nervous system and provide immediate relief during stressful moments. Choose a technique that resonates with you; one effective method is the 4-7-8 technique. Begin by sitting comfortably and closing your eyes. Inhale through your nose for a count of four, hold your breath for a count of seven, and exhale slowly through your mouth for a count of eight. Repeat this cycle for several minutes, focusing on the rhythm of your breath. If your mind wanders, gently bring your attention back to your breath. This exercise not only calms anxiety but also centers your focus. After practicing, take a moment to reflect on how your body feels and how your anxiety levels have shifted. Write down your insights in your journal, noting the effectiveness of these breathing techniques in managing stress.

Week 4: Trauma Exercises

As we enter Week 4, we will delve into trauma exercises that support healing and recovery.

Trauma can profoundly affect both the body and mind, often leading to feelings of disconnection and unease. This week, our focus will be on somatic practices that invite you to reconnect with your body and process traumatic experiences in a safe and supportive manner.

Through a combination of visualization, gentle movement, creative expression, and self-compassion techniques, you will create a nurturing space for healing. Each exercise is designed to facilitate a greater understanding of your trauma and promote emotional integration.

Allow yourself to approach this week with curiosity and compassion, embracing the path toward healing and wholeness as you engage with these practices.

Day 1: Somatic Experiencing

Today, we'll explore Somatic Experiencing to help process trauma. This technique focuses on reconnecting with bodily sensations to facilitate healing. Find a quiet and comfortable space where you can sit or lie down. Close your eyes and take a few deep breaths to ground yourself. Begin by tuning into your body and noticing any sensations—tightness, discomfort, or areas of relaxation. Instead of judging these feelings, allow yourself to experience them fully. If you notice discomfort, breathe into that area, acknowledging the sensation without the need to change it. Spend several minutes observing these sensations and how they shift or change. This practice encourages you to be present with your body, fostering a sense of safety. After the exercise, reflect on your experience. What sensations did you notice? How did this awareness affect your emotions? Write down your insights in your journal, emphasizing the importance of somatic awareness in trauma healing.

Day 2: Safe Space Visualization

Today's exercise involves creating a Safe Space Visualization to help you feel protected and at ease. This mental imagery can be a powerful tool for trauma recovery. Find a comfortable, quiet space where you can relax. Close your eyes and take a few deep breaths to center yourself. Imagine a safe place—this could be a cozy room, a peaceful forest, or anywhere you feel secure. Visualize the details: the colors, sounds, and scents. Feel the sensations of safety and comfort in this space. Allow yourself to fully immerse in this imagery, reinforcing the sense of protection it provides. When you encounter overwhelming emotions or triggers, you can revisit this safe space in your mind. After the exercise, take a moment to reflect on your experience. How did this visualization impact your sense of safety? Write down your thoughts in your journal, noting the significance of having a mental refuge during challenging moments.

Day 3: Titration Practice

For today's practice, we'll engage in Titration Practice to manage trauma-related emotions. This technique involves focusing on a small, manageable aspect of your trauma rather than overwhelming yourself with the entirety of it. Find a quiet space and take a few deep breaths to ground yourself. Identify a specific memory or feeling associated with your trauma that feels manageable to explore. Spend a few moments reflecting on this aspect, observing your thoughts and emotions as they arise. If at any point you feel overwhelmed, gently redirect your focus to a neutral or positive thought or image. This practice allows you to process trauma in smaller doses, helping to build resilience over time. After the exercise, reflect on your experience. How did it feel to engage with a small aspect of your trauma? What insights did you gain? Write down your reflections in your journal, emphasizing the importance of gradual processing in trauma recovery.

Day 4: Gentle Movement

Today, we'll focus on Gentle Movement as a way to release trauma

stored in the body. Gentle movement can promote healing and increase awareness of bodily sensations. Choose a space where you can move freely and comfortably. Begin with some gentle stretches or yoga poses, paying attention to how your body feels. Move slowly and intuitively, allowing your body to guide you. You might sway, rock, or perform simple movements that feel good. As you move, notice any emotions that arise. If you feel tension or discomfort, breathe into those areas and continue to move gently. This practice can help you reconnect with your body and release stored emotions. After your movement session, take a moment to reflect on your experience. What feelings or sensations arose during the practice? Write down your insights in your journal, emphasizing the role of movement in trauma recovery.

Day 5: Art Therapy

Today's exercise involves engaging in Art Therapy to express and process trauma. Artistic expression can be a powerful tool for healing, providing a non-verbal outlet for emotions. Gather some art supplies—this could be paper, paint, markers, or clay. Set aside time to create without judgment or expectation. Begin by focusing on a specific emotion or memory associated with your trauma. Allow your feelings to guide your artistic process. You might create an abstract piece representing your emotions or a more concrete representation of your experience. Remember, there's no right or wrong way to create—what matters is that you express yourself authentically. After your artistic session, take a moment to reflect on your creation. What emotions did you express through your art? How did the process feel? Write down your thoughts in your journal, emphasizing the therapeutic value of creative expression in trauma healing.

Day 6: Affirmative Touch

For today's practice, we'll explore Affirmative Touch as a way to promote self-compassion and healing. Touch can be a powerful tool for grounding and soothing the nervous system. Begin by finding a comfortable space to sit or lie down. Start by placing your hands on your heart or another area of your body where you feel tension. Close your eyes and take a few deep breaths, allowing your hands to provide warmth and comfort. As you hold this touch, repeat affirmations that resonate with you, such as "I am safe," "I am healing," or "I am enough." Feel the connection between your hands and your body, allowing this gentle touch to foster a sense of safety and compassion. Spend several minutes in this practice, focusing on how the touch affects your emotions. Afterward, reflect on your experience. How did the affirmative touch influence your emotional state? Write down your insights in your journal, emphasizing the significance of self-compassion in trauma recovery.

Day 7: Reflection and Integration

For our final exercise this week, we'll engage in Reflection and Integration to consolidate your learnings. Take time to review your journal entries and experiences from the past week. Reflect on the exercises you practiced and any insights or emotions that arose during this time. Consider how these practices contributed to your understanding of trauma and its effects on your body and mind. Write about your feelings in a summary entry, emphasizing any shifts in your perspective or emotional state. You might also want to set intentions for how you can continue incorporating these practices into your daily life. This reflection will help reinforce your progress and solidify your commitment to healing. Remember, healing from trauma is a journey, and it's essential to celebrate your growth along the way.

Meet the Author

Anika Sullivan is a trauma-informed somatic healing practitioner, journal designer, and mental wellness educator with a deep passion for integrating mind, body, and spirit in the healing process. With a background in psychology, expressive arts, and body-centered therapy, she creates compassionate tools that help people reconnect with themselves from the inside out.

Her work is rooted in the belief that the body holds wisdom words cannot always express, and that healing is not linear, it's embodied. Anika's journaling frameworks combine gentle inquiry, nervous system awareness, and emotional safety to help readers process their stories at a pace that honors their capacity.

When she's not writing or teaching, Anika spends her time in nature, practicing breathwork, and curating spaces that invite stillness and self-trust.